ENGLISH G

access 1|2

ENGLISCH FÜR DAZ-LERNENDE

 ONLINE-Angebot

mit Audios und
Lösungen online

Cornelsen

Content

Content

1 Welcome to our class

Good morning.

Welcome to our class.

Nice to meet you.

My name is Mr Chan.

I'm your English teacher.

classmate

Hello.

Hi.

What's your name?

I'm Jill.

Are you a student too?

No, I'm not.

Where are you from?

I'm from Syria.

My poster is about Syria.

How old are you?

I'm 13 years old.

What's your favourite music?

My favourite music is hip-hop.

Rap and hip-hop are OK.

But my favourite music is house.

There's a green door.

There are lockers.

school

Let's go.

→ My Words, pp. 14–15

1 Welcome to our class

a 🔊1 📖 Look at page 4. Listen and read.
b 📖 ✂ Read the texts. Match the pictures to the texts.

12 twelve
13 thirteen
14 fourteen
20 twenty

I'm Jill. I'm 20 years old. I'm from England.	My name is Yero. I'm 12 years old. I'm from Guinea.	I'm Olga. I'm 14 years old. I'm from Russia.	My name is Mo. I'm 13 years old. I'm from Syria.

2 What about you?

a 🖊 Write about yourself:
– What's your name?
– How old are you?
– Where are you from?

b 👥 💬 Ask and answer the questions with a partner.

your picture	I'm _____ _____ _____

TIP: Change the green words in the sentences from 1b:
I'm Jill.
→ I'm Adnan.

3 Your classmates

a 📖 Look and read.
b 🖊 Write about a student from your class and draw a picture.

This is Jill.
She's 20.
She's from England.
She's a language assistant.

This is Mo.
He's 13.
He's from Syria.
He's a student.

She is a student.

He is 12.

TIP: Change the green words in the sentences:
This is Yero.
→ This is Jasmin.

4 Act out the dialogue

a 🔊1 📖 Listen to and read the dialogue on page 4 again.
b 👥 💬 Act out the dialogue in a group. Or record it.

→ My Words, pp. 14–15

1 Welcome to our class

1 Personal pronouns

🔊2 📖 💬 Listen and read. Listen again and repeat.

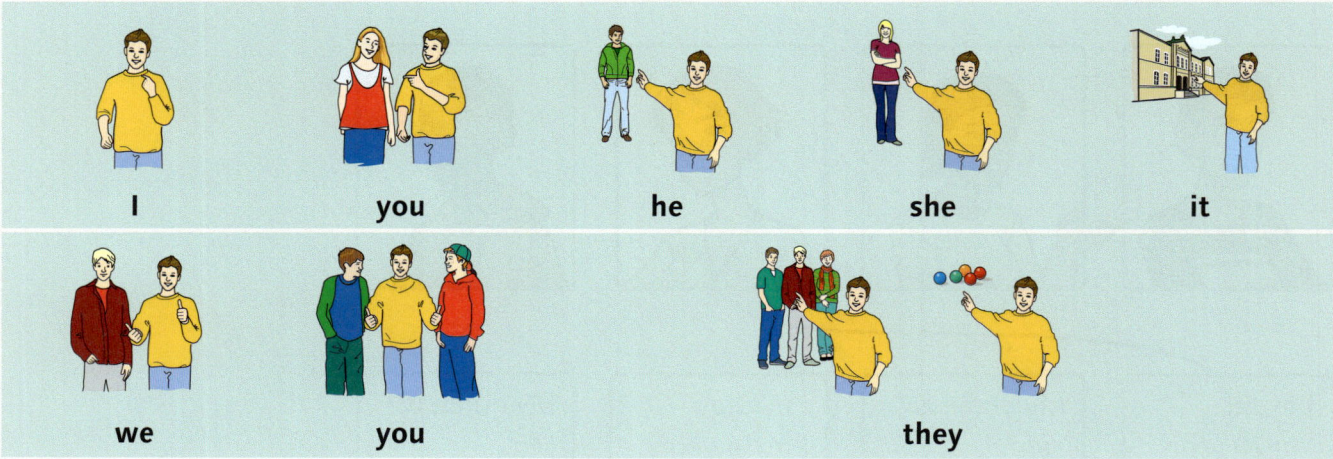

| I | you | he | she | it |

| we | you | they |

2 The verb *be* in the present tense: positive statements

a 🔊3 📖 💬 Listen and read. Listen again and repeat.

| I'm from England. | You're from Syria. | He's … | She's … | It's … |
| I am … | You are … | He is … | She is … | It is … |

| We're … | You're … | They're … |
| We are … | You are … | They are … |

b 🔊4 📖 Listen and read.

Hi, Mo. Meet Lydia and Adrian. They're from Georgia.

Lydia and Adrian, meet Mo. He's from Syria.

Nice to meet you, Lydia and Adrian.

Hello, Mo.

Nice to meet you.

c 👥 💬 Act out the dialogue from 2b in a group. Make your own dialogues.

Afghanistan • Croatia • Denmark • Eritrea • France • Germany • Georgia • Iran • Iraq • Italy • Lebanon • Nigeria • Portugal • Russia • Serbia • Somalia • Spain • Sweden • Turkey • the USA • …

d ✎ Complete the sentences.

| He (2 x) • She • It • We • They | **+** | 's (is) • 're (are) |

1 This is Yero. *He's*___ from Guinea.

2 This is Olga and this is Yero.

_____ in my class.

3 Olga and I are friends.

_____ in the classroom.

4 This is Jill. _____ from England.

5 This is Mr Chan. _____ my English teacher.

6 This is my favourite poster. _____ about Syria.

3 The verb *be* in the present tense: negative statements

🔊5 📑 💬 Listen and read. Listen again and repeat.

I'm not 15. I am not 15.	You're not … You are not …	He isn't … He is not …	She isn't … She is not …	It isn't … It is not …
We aren't … We are not …	You aren't … You are not …	They aren't … They are not …		

4 The verb *be* in the present tense: questions and short answers

a 📑 Read the boxes.

| Am I 14?
Are you …?
Is he/she/it …?
Are we …?
Are you …?
Are they …? | Yes, | I am.
you are.
he/she/it is.
we are.
you are.
they are. | No, | I'm not.
you aren't.
he/she/it isn't.
we aren't.
you aren't.
they aren't. | **Questions with question words:**
What's (=is) your name?
Where are you from?
→ Module 3, p. 33
(questions) |

b 🔊6 ✎ Listen. Then write six or more questions in your exercise book. Answer the questions.

| Are you
Is Jill
Is Yero | from England • from Russia •
12 years old • Mo's classmate •
a student • a teacher • …? |

Are you from England? – No, I'm not.

b 👥 💬 Ask and answer your questions with a partner.

Numbers:
0 zero, oh
1 one
2 two
3 three
4 four
5 five
6 six
7 seven
8 eight
9 nine
10 ten
11 eleven
12 twelve
13 thirteen
14 fourteen
15 fifteen
16 sixteen
17 seventeen
18 eighteen
19 nineteen
20 twenty

What's your telephone number?

You write	You say
0	oh
00	double oh
99	double nine

1 Numbers

a 🔊7 📖 Listen to and read the numbers in the margin.

b 🔊8 ✎ Listen and write down the telephone numbers.

0044 _____

c 👥✎💬 Write down two numbers or telephone numbers. Ask and answer with a partner. Write down and check your partner's numbers.

Me: _____

_____

My partner: _____

_____

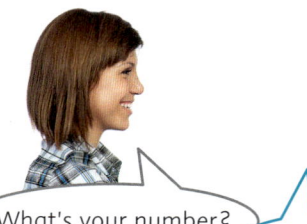

What's your number?

It's 1719411351.

d ✎ Complete the crossword puzzle.

1 one, ... , five, seven

2 ... , four, six, eight

3 zero, six, twelve, ...

4 five, eight, ... , fourteen

5 eleven, nine, seven, ...

6 eight, eleven, fourteen, ...

	T	H			

2 Thinking about languages

a ✎💬 Write and say the numbers 1–10 in your language(s).

b 👥💬 Talk to your classmates and find out about other languages.

	English	Arabic	Fula	Russian	...
1	one	واحد	goo	один	...
2	two	اثنان	zizi	два	

go'o

wahid

adin

→ Numbers, p. 111
→ My Words, pp. 14–15

3 Colours

a 🔊9 📑 Listen to and read the colour words in the margin.

b 🔊10 ✏ Listen and colour the pens.

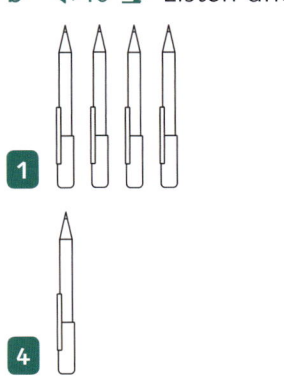

1 **2** **3**

4 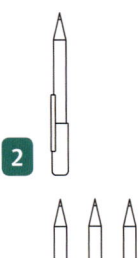 **5** **6**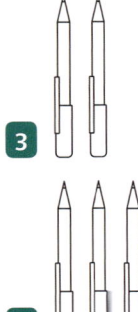

c 📑 ✏ Find the colour words and mark them.

N	C	O	H	B	O	G	R	E	Y
A	R	A	L	L	V	D	Y	O	K
C	Y	L	P	U	R	P	L	E	Y
R	E	D	I	E	B	L	A	C	K
H	L	E	N	G	R	E	E	N	A
H	L	L	K	U	O	W	T	E	N
D	O	L	L	G	W	H	I	T	E
H	W	O	R	A	N	G	E	R	P

black • blue • brown • green • ~~grey~~ • orange • pink • purple • red • white • yellow

d 🔊11 ✏ Listen and colour the things.

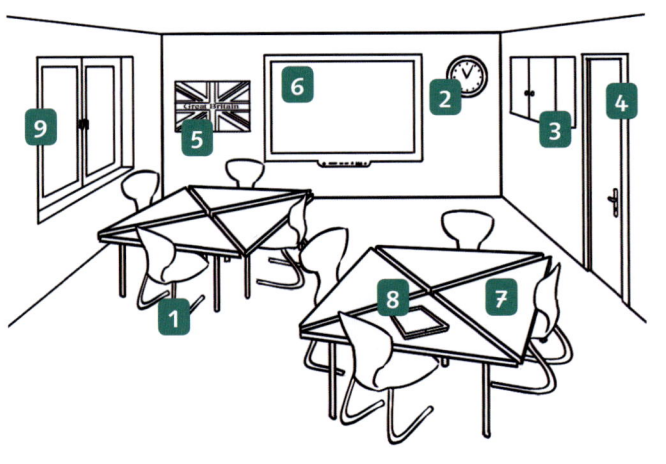

1 a chair
2 a clock
3 a cupboard
4 a door
5 a poster
6 a smartboard
7 a table
8 a tablet
9 a window

e 🔊11 ✏ Listen again and write sentences 1–9 in your exercise book.

1. The chair is …

Colours:
black ⬤
blue 🔵
brown 🟤
green 🟢
grey ⬤
orange 🟠
pink 🟣
purple 🟣
red 🔴
white ⚪
yellow 🟡

Things in the classroom:
chair
clock
cupboard
door
smartboard
table
tablet
window

English and German

The door is red.
Die Tür ist rot.

The chair is blue.
Der Stuhl ist blau

The smartboard is black.
Das Smartboard ist schwarz.

→ My Words, pp. 14–15

1 Welcome to our class

Short and long forms
short: There**'s** a table.
long: There **is** a table.

Singular and plural
There**'s** (= **is**) a table.
There **are** books.

book
pen

singular	plural
	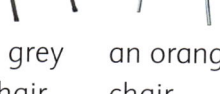
one pen	two pen**s**
chair	chair**s**
book	book**s**
table	table**s**
glass	glass**es**

the plural: noun + **s**

new ↔ old
full ↔ empty
glass

a or an?
Check how you **say**
the next word:
a red chair
a full glass
a tablet
an orange chair
an empty glass

With **A, E, I, O, U**
you say **an**.

→ Sounds, p.110

⊞
There's a book.
There are books.

⊟
There isn't a book.
There aren't any books.

→ My Words, pp.14–15

4 There are two orange chairs

a 🔊12 📑 Listen and read.

There's a smartboard.
There's a white table.
There are two orange chairs.
There are five books.
There are …

> books • chairs • a clock •
> a door • pens • a table • tablets

b 🔊12 ✏ Listen again and look. Write in your exercise book:

There's …	There are …
There's a smartboard.	There are two orange chairs.

5 When to say *a* or *an*

a 🔊13 📑 💬 Listen and read. Listen again and repeat.

a grey chair · an orange chair · a full glass · an empty glass · a new book · an old book

b ✏ Write *a* or *an*.

1 There's _____ old clock.
2 There's _____ new smartboard.
3 There's _____ yellow table.
4 There's _____ empty locker.

c 💬 Practise a and b. Read aloud and record it.

6 There aren't any empty glasses

a 📑 💬 Look and read. Read aloud.

There isn't an orange table.
There's a red table.
There aren't any empty glasses.
There are full glasses.
There aren't any new books.
There are old books.

b ✏ Write six or more sentences about your school in your exercise book.

There's	English dictionaries • lockers •	in my classroom.
There isn't	new chairs • nice students •	at my school.
There are	nice teachers • a cupboard •	
There aren't any	a smartboard • …	

There aren't any lockers at my school …

7 Is there a smartboard?

a 🔊14 📖 Listen and read.

Mr Chan: Well, Yero. Let's see …
What's in our new classroom?
Is there a smartboard?
Yero: Yes, there is, Mr Chan.
Mr Chan: Are there any tablets?
Yero: Yes, there are.
Mr Chan: Are there any dictionaries?
Yero: No, there aren't.

b ✏ Mark the questions and the answers.

c ✏ Write six or more questions about your school in your exercise book.

Is there a/an	canteen • English dictionary •	in our
Are there any	library • red pens • students •	classroom?
	swimming pool • nice teachers • …	at our school?

d 👥💬✏ Ask a partner and write down your partner's answers.

e 👥💬 Record your questions and answers.

8 Thinking about languages

a 📖 Look and read.

Hi, Tom.

friend

Hello, Dad.

parent

Good morning, Mrs Adam.

teacher

b 👥💬 How do you say 'hello' to friends, parents and teachers in your language(s)? Talk to your classmates.

in my classroom
at my school
a nice student / teacher

Singular and plural
one dictionary
two dictionaries
y → ies

Is there a smartboard?
Yes, there is.
No, there isn't.

Are there any dictionaries?
Yes, there are.
No, there aren't.

TIP: Look up words in an online dictionary or in the English-German dictionary for this workbook.

friend
parents (pl)

→ My Words, pp. 14–15

1 Learning words

a   Read. Then look at the word list *My Words* on pages 14–15.

English	German	My notes
Nice to meet you.	Schön, dich/Sie kennen zu lernen.	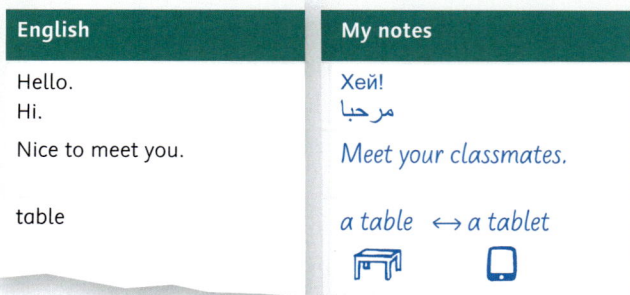
Welcome to our class.	Willkommen in unserer Klasse.	
Hello.	Hallo.	
Hi.	Hi.	

b   Add to the word list on pages 14–15:

1. Write words in your language or other languages.
2. Write English examples.
3. Draw pictures.

English	My notes
Hello.	Хей!
Hi.	مرحبا
Nice to meet you.	*Meet your classmates.*
table	*a table ↔ a tablet*

c   Practise your words every day.

2 Find your way of learning

Read the tips and try them out:

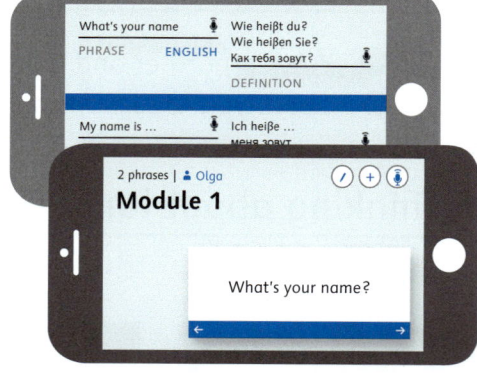

1. Write difficult words and phrases on notes and put them up.

2. Make vocabulary cards with a vocabulary app:
   – Write the new words and phrases.
   – Write the words and phrases in German and your language(s).
   – You can add pictures.
   – Practise on your smartphone.

Checkpoint

1 ✐ Mark the words with the right colours.

○ blue ○ brown ○ green ○ orange
○ purple ○ yellow ○ grey ○ black
○ red ○ pink ○ white

2 🔊15 ✐ Listen and mark the right numbers.

1

1	2	3	4	5
6	7	8	9	10
11	12	13	14	15

2

2	4	6	8	10
12	14	16	18	20
10	0	1	5	7

3

3	5	8	1	15
11	13	6	2	4
7	14	18	9	6

3 ✐ Write about yourself.

– What's your name?

– How old are you?

– What's your favourite music?

– Are you a teacher?

4 ✐ Look at the pictures. Complete the sentences.

1 _____ a blue table.

2 _____ a green chair.

3 _____ empty glasses.

4 _____ full glasses.

5 ✓ Tick the right answers.

1 Are you a student?

○ No, I'm not. ○ Yes, you are. ○ Yes, I am. ○ Yes, he is.

2 Is your English teacher from Germany?

○ No, she isn't. ○ No, he isn't. ○ Yes, he is. ○ Yes, she is.

3 Is there a smartboard in your classroom?

○ Yes, there are. ○ No, there aren't. ○ Yes, there is. ○ No, there isn't.

1 Welcome to our class

English	German	My notes
Nice to meet you.	Schön, dich/Sie kennen zu lernen.	
Welcome to our class.	Willkommen in unserer Klasse.	
Hello. Hi.	Hallo. Hi.	
Good morning.	Guten Morgen.	
What's your name?	Wie heißt du?/ Wie heißen Sie?	
My name is Mr Chan. **I'm** your English teacher.	Ich heiße Herr Chan. Ich bin dein/euer Englischlehrer.	
How old are you?	Wie alt bist du?/ Wie alt sind Sie?	
I'm 13 (years old).	Ich bin 13 (Jahre alt).	
Where are you from?	Woher kommst du?/ Woher kommen Sie?	
I'm from Syria.	Ich komme aus Syrien.	
My poster is about Syria.	Mein Poster zeigt Syrien.	
What's your favourite music?	Was ist deine/Ihre Lieblingsmusik?	
My favourite music is hip-hop.	Meine Lieblingsmusik ist Rap.	
Rap and hip-hop are **OK**. **But** my favourite music is …	Rap und Hip-Hop sind okay. Aber meine Lieblingsmusik ist …	
There's (= **there is**) a door. **There are** lockers.	Es gibt eine Tür./Da ist … Es gibt Schließfächer.	
Are you a student too?	Bist du auch ein/e Schüler/in?/Sind Sie …?	
Are you from England? Yes, I am./No, I'm not. Yes, we are./No, we aren't.	Bist du aus England?/ Seid ihr …?/Sind Sie …? Ja./Nein.	
at my school **in** my classroom	in/an meiner Schule in meinem Klassenzimmer	
Let's go.	Lass(t) uns gehen.	

My Words

English	German	My notes

Colours (Farben)
● **black** schwarz ● **blue** blau ● **brown** braun ● **green** grün
● **grey** grau ● **orange** orange ● **pink** rosa, pink
● **purple** lila ● **red** rot ○ **white** weiß ● **yellow** gelb

There isn't a blue chair.	Es gibt keinen blauen Stuhl.
There aren't any red chairs.	Es gibt keine roten Stühle.
What's your (telephone) number?	Wie ist deine Nummer?

The numbers from 0 to 20 (Die Zahlen von 0 bis 20)
0 zero, 1 one, 2 two, 3 three, 4 four, 5 five, 6 six, 7 seven,
8 eight, 9 nine, 10 ten, 11 eleven, 12 twelve, 13 thirteen,
14 fourteen, 15 fifteen, 16 sixteen, 17 seventeen,
18 eighteen, 19 nineteen, 20 twenty   → Numbers, p. 109

People:	**Personen:**
teacher	der Lehrer/die Lehrerin
classmate	der Mitschüler/ die Mitschülerin
student	der Schüler/die Schülerin
friend	der Freund/die Freundin
parents (pl)	die Eltern (Pl.)

Things in the classroom:	**Dinge im Klassenzimmer:**
pen	der Kugelschreiber, der Stift
chair	der Stuhl
clock	die Uhr
cupboard	der Schrank
smartboard	das Smartboard
table	der Tisch
tablet	das Tablet
window	das Fenster
an **old** book a **new** book	ein altes Buch ein neues Buch
a **full** glass an **empty** glass	ein volles Glas ein leeres Glas
dictionary, pl dictionaries	das Wörterbuch

2 My school week

It's 8 o'clock.

It's Tuesday.

What do we do every Tuesday?

I teach English every Tuesday.

(to) teach English

(to) learn English

(to) go to the computer room

(to) take a test

sometimes

Look at the timetable, please.

I like PE too.

I don't like history.

Subjects:
English
maths
PE
history

Open your books at page 42.

Can you read task 1, please?

(to) play football

(to) study English

(to) do homework

after school
on Wednesdays
at the weekend

always
never
usually
every day

→ My Words, pp. 28–29

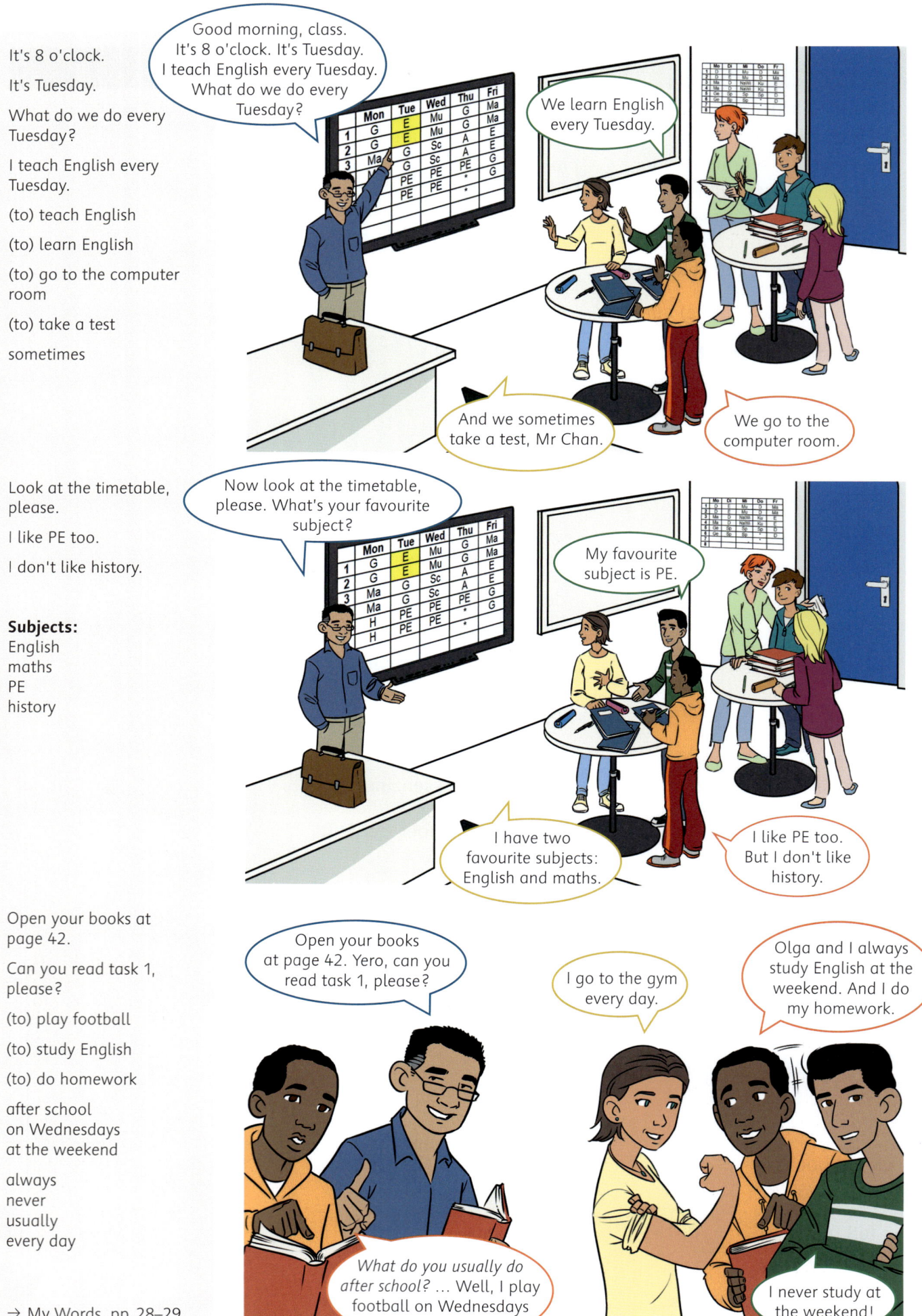

1 Every Tuesday

a 🔊16 📑 Look at page 4. Listen and read.

b 📑 💬 Read aloud.

TIP: You can read or act out the dialogue with your classmates. One classmate is Mo, one classmate is Jill, etc.

2 Right or wrong?

a ✏️ 📑 Tick the right answers. Check your answers on page 16.

◯ It's 10 o'clock.

✔️ It's Tuesday.

◯ The students open their books.

◯ They go to the computer room.

◯ Yero studies English at the weekend.

◯ Mr Chan teaches English.

TIP:
1. Read the sentences.
2. Read or listen to the text again.
3. Tick or match the sentences.
4. Check your answers.

b ✂️ 📑 Match the sentence parts. Check your answers on page 16.

1 Yero

2 Mo

3 Mr Chan

4 Olga

A teaches English.

B goes to the gym every day.

C likes history.

D plays football.

3 School things

a 🔊17 💬 Look at the pictures. Listen and repeat.

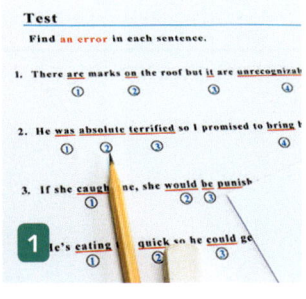
1

2

3

4

5

6

School things:
computer
exercise book
pen
pencil
test
timetable

TIP: Label the things in your classroom. Add more labels every day. Do the same at home.

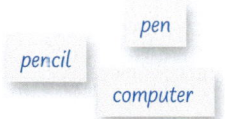
pen
pencil
computer

Look up new words in an online dictionary.

→ p.26 (Online dictionaries and apps)

b ✏️ Look at the pictures again. Number the words (1–6).

◯ a timetable

① a test

◯ a computer

◯ a pencil

◯ an exercise book

◯ a pen

→ My Words, pp. 28–29

2 My school week

1 The simple present: positive statements

a ▤ Read the boxes.

I You We You They	learn English.
He/She/It	learns English.

The simple present has one form for *I, you, we* and *they*. For he, she, it you add an -s.

I go to the gym every day.
Mr Chan teaches English every Tuesday.
The class sometimes takes a test.
Mo never studies at the weekend.

You use the simple present to say what you usually do or what usually happens.
Signal words: every day, on Wednesdays, always, sometimes, usually, never, …

b ✎ Complete the sentences with *learn or learns*.

1 They _learn_ English every day.

2 He never _____ English at the weekend.

3 We _____ English every Tuesday.

4 You always _____ English at the weekend.

5 She _____ English on Wednesdays.

6 I sometimes _____ English with my friend.

c ✎ Mark the signal words in sentences 1–6.

2 The simple present: special verbs

a ▤ Read the box.

⚠ Be careful with the spelling of these verbs:
teach: he/she/it teaches
go, do: he/she/it goes, does
study: he/she/it studies
have: he/she/it has

be: I am
we/you/they are
he/she/it is

→ Module 1, p. 6 (be)

b ✎ ◀))18 ▤ Complete the sentences. Listen and check.

1 Mr Chan _____ (teach) English every Tuesday.

2 The students _____ (look) at the timetable every day.

3 Mo never _____ (study) at the weekend.

4 Olga _____ (go) to the gym every day.

5 They sometimes _____ (take) a test on Tuesdays.

6 Olga _____ (have) two favourite subjects: English and maths.

7 Mo _____ (do) his homework after school.

3 The simple present: negative statements

a 📖 ✏ Read the boxes. Then mark *doesn't* or *don't* in the sentences.

I You We You They	don't study.
He/She/It	doesn't study.

In negative statements in the simple present you use don't for *I*, *you*, *we*, *they*. You use doesn't for he, she, it.

After don't and doesn't you use the infinitive of the verb:
⊞ Mr Chan teaches English.
⊟ Mr Chan doesn't teach history.

1 Mr Chan and Mrs Kern **doesn't/don't** teach on Sundays.
2 Mo **doesn't/don't** study at the weekend.
3 Jill **doesn't/don't** go to school.

4 We **doesn't/don't** have PE on Fridays.
5 I **doesn't/don't** like school.
6 Olga **doesn't/don't** play football.

4 *Can* and *can't (cannot)*

a 📖 ✏ Read the boxes. Then complete the sentences with *can* or *can't*.

Positive statements	
I/You He/She/It We/You/They	can play.

Negative statements	
I/You He/She/It We/You/They	can't (= cannot) play.

1 He _____ go to school.
2 She _____ play football.

3 He _____ do his homework.
4 She _____ open the door.

b 🔊 19 📖 Listen and check.
c ✏ What can or can't you do? Write four or more sentences.

I can I can't	do my homework after school • go to the gym on Mondays • play football/ basketball/… • read an English book • study at the weekend • …

I can't play football. I can ...

d 👥 💬 Compare your sentences with a partner.

School starts at 8 o'clock.
(to) wear your own clothes
(to) wear a school uniform
(to) get a mark

1 Schools in Britain and Germany

a 📖 🔊20 Look and read. Then listen to Jill.

b 🔊20 ✏ Listen again. Write *G* for Germany and *B* for Britain.

> In Britain students wear school uniforms.

1	Students wear school uniforms.	Ⓑ
2	School starts at 8 o'clock.	◯
3	Students get marks A–F.	◯
4	Students wear their own clothes.	◯
5	School starts at 8:45.	◯
6	Students get marks 1–6.	◯

1 (sehr gut!)

2 What can you say about your school in Germany?

School finishes at 3:15.
(to) speak English/
German

a ✏ Write six or more sentences in your exercise book.

At our school we (don't)	have a computer room • wear a school uniform / our own clothes • get marks 1–6 • speak English/ German with our friends • take tests every week • …

Our school	starts at 8:00 • usually finishes at 3:15 • is great/OK/nice • …

At our school we get marks 1–6. We don't …

> **TIP:** You can look up more words in a dictionary.
> → p. 26 (How to use a dictionary)

→ My Words, pp. 28–29

b 👥 💬 Compare your sentences with a partner.

3 Thinking about cultures

a ✏️ What do you know about schools in other countries? Write down ideas.

*In Guinea school usually starts at ...
Students usually wear ...*

b 👥💬 Talk to your classmates.
c ✋✏️ Make a poster about schools in one country. Present it to the class.

School in Guinea
- school starts at 9.00
- students often wear school uniforms
- students get marks A–F

TIP: You can use words and sentences from page 20. You can look up more words in a dictionary.

→ p. 26 (How to use a dictionary)

4 The days of the week

a 🔊21 🔲 Listen to and read the days of the week in the margin.
b 🔊21 💬 Listen again and repeat.

Days of the week:
Monday
Tuesday
Wednesday
Thursday
Friday
Saturday
Sunday

(to) use a computer

5 Mo's week

🔊22 ✏️ Listen to Mo. Write the days into the puzzle.
Then complete Mo's speech bubble.

1 Mo does his English homework on [...] .

2 He studies with his friend on [...] .

3 He goes to school at 9:50 on [...] .

4 He goes to the gym on [...] .

5 He has English and German on [...] .

6 He can use his brother's computer on [...] .

The best day of the week is

S _ _ _ _ _ _ !

→ My Words, pp. 28–29

Numbers:
20 twenty
21 twenty-one
22 twenty-two
23 twenty-three
24 twenty-four
25 twenty-five
26 twenty-six
27 twenty-seven
28 twenty-eight
29 twenty-nine
30 thirty
31 thirty-one
…

It's the same for 40, 50, 60, 70, 80 and 90.

40 forty	70 seventy
50 fifty	80 eighty
60 sixty	90 ninety

→ Numbers, p. 111

6 Numbers from 20 to 99

a ◀)23 📖 Listen to and read the numbers in the margin.

b ◀)23 💬 Listen again and repeat.

c Match the numbers to the words.

86 · 70 · 34 · 53 · 91

forty-five
thirty-four
thirty-three
seventy
ninety-nine
eighty-six
forty-seven
ninety-one
fifty-three
sixty-eight

33 · 99 · 45 · 47 · 68

d ◀)24 ✏ Listen and write the numbers in words.

27 • 45 • 55 • 78 • 86 • 92

1 *twenty-seven*

2 _____

3 _____

4 _____

5 _____

6 _____

7 What's the time?

a ◀)25 💬 Listen and repeat.

**What's the time?
It's …**

 ten o'clock

 ten fifteen
quarter past ten

 ten thirty
half past ten

 ten forty-five
quarter to eleven

 ten fifty-five
five to eleven

 ten oh five
five past ten

→ My Words, pp. 28–29

1     4    7

2     5    8

3    6

b ◀)25 ✏ Listen again and complete the sentences.

1 It's *eight* o'clock.

2 It's ten past _____.

3 It's quarter past _____.

4 It's _____ past _____.

5 It's half past _____.

6 It's quarter to _____.

7 It's _____ to one.

8 It's _____ to _____.

8 A timetable

a 🔊26 📖 ✏️ Look at the timetable and listen.
What are Jill's favourite subjects? Tick.

⬭ PE ⬭ science

⬭ ICT ⬭ art

This is a timetable from my old school in England.

Lesson/Time		Mon	Tue	Wed	Thu	Fri
	8.45–9.00			Assembly		
1	9.00–10.00	PE	English	Art	English	Maths
2	10.00–11.00	PE	English	English	Geography	ICT
	11.00–11.20			Break		
3	11.20–12.20	Science	Music	Science	History	German

School subjects:
art
English
German
geography
history
ICT
music
maths
PE
science

lesson
break

b 📖 ✏️ Look at the timetable again. Tick the right answers.

⬭ School starts at 8:45.

⬭ Lesson 1 on Monday is maths.

⬭ The class takes a break at 10:15.

⬭ Lesson 3 on Wednesday is science.

⬭ There are no art lessons.

⬭ Lessons 1 and 2 on Tuesday are English.

c ✏️ Complete the sentences.

1 **PE** _____ is from 9 to 11 o'clock on Monday.   from 9 to 11 o'clock

2 _____ is at 9 o'clock on Friday.

3 _____ is at 11:20 on Monday and Wednesday.

4 _____ is at 10 o'clock on Thursday.

d 👥 ✏️ 💬 Write your timetable in English. Talk to a partner about
your timetable. You can use sentences from b and c.

→ My Words, pp. 28–29

Listen, please.
Read page 32.

English and German
Listen, please.
Hör bitte zu!
Hört bitte zu!
Hören Sie bitte zu!

→ Classroom English,
   p. 112

Can you spell that word,
please?

The alphabet:
Aa Bb Cc Dd Ed Ff Gg
Hh Ii Jj Kk Ll Mm Nn
Oo Pp Qq Rr Ss Tt Uu
Vv Ww Xx Yy Zz

→ Alphabet, p. 110

You write	You say
ss	double s
oo	double oh

English and German
I can read this text.
Ich kann diesen
Text lesen.

9 Classroom talk

🔊 27 📑 🖊 What do you hear? Listen, read and tick.

1 ⚪ Open your books at page 3.   ⚪ Open your tablets, please.
2 ⚪ The lesson starts at 12:20.   ⚪ The lesson finishes at 12:20.
3 ⚪ Read page 32 in your   ⚪ Read page 32 in your
     science book.   history book.
4 ⚪ Look at the timetable.   ⚪ Look at page 99.
5 ⚪ Look, please.   ⚪ Listen, please.

10 Can you spell that word, please?

a 🔊 28 📑 Listen to and read the alphabet in the margin.
b 🔊 29 📑 💬 Listen to and read the alphabet in sound groups. Repeat.

A H J K   B C D E G P T V   I Y
Q U W   F L M N S X Z   O R

c 🔊 30 🖊 Listen and write down the words.

1 p _ _ _ _ _ _   2 _ _ _ _ _ _   3 _ _ _ _ _ _ _   4 _ _ _ _ _ _

d 💬 🔊 31 Spell the words. Then listen and check.

1 favourite   3 classroom   5 science
2 uniform   4 lesson   6 school

11 Can a teacher wear a school uniform?

🖊 Write correct sentences with *can* and *can't*.

1 geography. | teach | can't | A maths teacher

   A maths teacher _____

2 can't | The students | go | on a Sunday. | to school

   _____

3 English | after school. | can | They | study

   _____

4 wear | A teacher | can't | a school uniform.

   _____

→ My Words, pp. 28–29

12 Write about your school week

✏️ ✋ There's a new student in your class.
Write a letter or make a video blog.
Tell the student about:
– your class and classroom
– your school week
– your favourite subjects
– your teachers
– what you and your classmates
  do after school

> Welcome to our
> class, Bilal!

TIP: Change the green words in the text:
Our classroom is nice.
→ Our classroom is OK.

Welcome to our class, Bilal!

Our class
In our class we have twenty-one students.
Our classroom is nice.
We have a smartboard and a computer.
But we don't have tablets.

→ Numbers, p. 111

→ Module 1, p. 15
(things in the classroom)

Our school week
School usually starts at 7:40.
We have two breaks in the morning,
at 9:30 and at 11:20.
School usually finishes at 3:15.
On Fridays it finishes at 2:30.

> new • OK • old • …

> English dictionaries •
> new tables • …

→ p. 22 (time)

We go to the computer room on Tuesdays
and Fridays. We often watch videos.
And we sometimes make videos.

> Monday • Tuesday • …

→ p. 21 (days)

My favourite subject is PE. ❤️
I like geography too.
What are your favourite subjects?

> take tests • listen to
> music • make posters •
> act out dialogues • …

→ p. 23 (subjects)

Our teachers
Mr Kienbaum teaches English.
Mrs Weiler teaches German and maths.

> art • history • ICT • …

After school
Our class is really nice. After school we
sometimes meet in the school garden
and study. You can come with us!

Your classmate
Miriam

> do homework • study
> English/German/… •
> meet in the school
> canteen/cafe/… •
> play football • …

TIP: You can look
up more words in an
online dictionary.

→ p. 26 (Online
dictionaries
and apps)

→ Alphabet, p. 110

TIP: There's an online English-German dictionary for this workbook.

1 How to use a dictionary

a Read the example from an English-German dictionary.

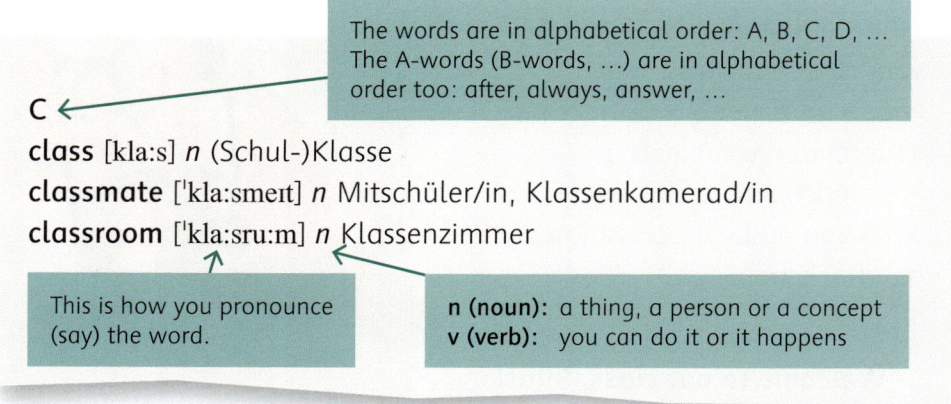

The words are in alphabetical order: A, B, C, D, …
The A-words (B-words, …) are in alphabetical order too: after, always, answer, …

C

class [kla:s] *n* (Schul-)Klasse
classmate ['kla:smeɪt] *n* Mitschüler/in, Klassenkamerad/in
classroom ['kla:sru:m] *n* Klassenzimmer

This is how you pronounce (say) the word.

n (noun): a thing, a person or a concept
v (verb): you can do it or it happens

b Write these words in alphabetical order.

clothes • test • computer • pen

1 _____   2 _____   3 _____   4 _____

c Find these words in a dictionary. Write *n* (noun) or *v* (verb).

playground (*n*)   training ( )   invitation ( )

celebrate ( )   look *sth.* up ( )   meet ( )

2 Online dictionaries and apps

a Look at the online dictionary and read the boxes.

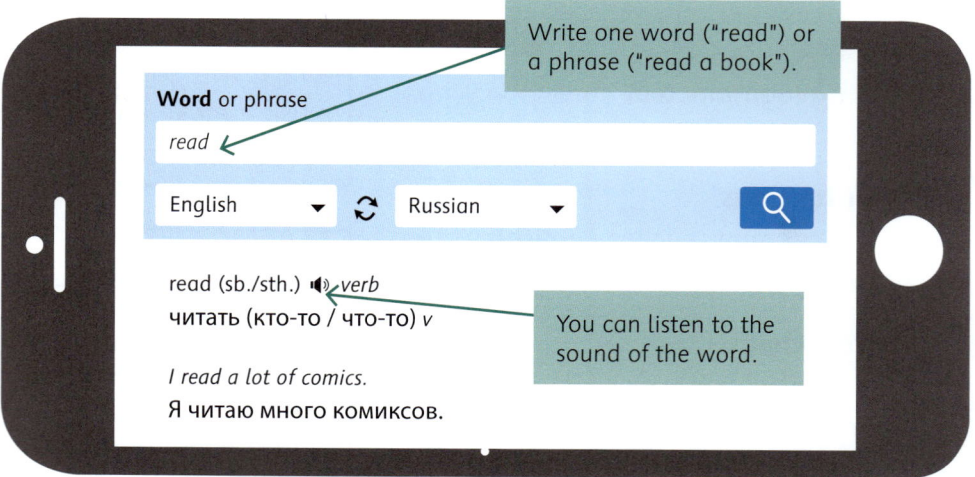

Write one word ("read") or a phrase ("read a book").

Word or phrase

read

English ▼   ⟳   Russian ▼   🔍

read (sb./sth.) ◀) *verb*
читать (кто-то / что-то) *v*

You can listen to the sound of the word.

I read a lot of comics.
Я читаю много комиксов.

TIP: There are lots of free online dictionaries and apps.

b Look up the verb *read* in an online dictionary.
Write down the meaning in German and in your language(s).

read sth. *v*   German: _____

Your language(s): _____

Checkpoint

1 ✎ Look at the pictures and write the school subjects.

_____ → 🌍   🏛 ← _____

_____ → 🎨   🇩🇪 ← _____

_____ → 🏀   🔬 ← _____

😊 ☐
😐 ☐
☹ ☐

2 ✎ What's the time? Tick the right answers.

1 12:15 ☐ quarter to twelve ☐ twelve past ten ☐ quarter past twelve

2 3:30 ☐ half past four ☐ half past three ☐ half past two

3 6:45 ☐ quarter past six ☐ half past seven ☐ quarter to seven

4 9.55 ☐ five to ten ☐ five past ten ☐ five to nine

😊 ☐
😐 ☐
☹ ☐

3 📖 ✎ Complete the text. Use the simple present.

Jo, Dev and Milly _____ (go) to Mercy School. School usually _____ (start) at 9 o'clock. The students at Mercy _____ (wear) school uniforms. They _____ (not wear) their own clothes. Milly _____ (not like) the school uniform. On Monday Jo _____ (have) two German lessons. Dev and Milly _____ (not have) German. They _____ (learn) French. In lessons 5 and 6 Mrs Fine _____ (teach) ICT. She always _____ (go) to the computer room with the class. School _____ (finish) at 3.30. After school Dev and Milly usually _____ (do) their homework. Jo _____ (play) football. He usually _____ (do) his homework after football training.

😊 ☐
😐 ☐
☹ ☐

4 📖 ✎ What can (✓) or can't (✗) they do? Read and write.

1 Taio and Ava _____

2 Taio _____

3 Ava _____

4 Taio and Ava _____

	T	A
speak German	✓	✓
spell 'geography'	✗	✓
take the maths test	✗	✗

😊 ☐
😐 ☐
☹ ☐

2 My school week

English	German	My notes
Open your books at page 42.	Schlagt eure Bücher auf Seite 42 auf.	
Look at the timetable.	Schaue auf den Stundenplan./ Schaut …	
Read page 32.	Lies Seite 32/Lest …	
Can you read task 1, please?	Kannst du bitte Aufgabe 1 vorlesen?/Könnt ihr …?	
Can you spell that word, please?	Kannst du bitte das Wort buchstabieren?/ Könnt ihr …?	
Listen, please.	Hör bitte zu!/Hört bitte zu!	
(to) take a test	einen Test schreiben	
(to) do homework	Hausaufgaben machen	
(to) play football	Fußball spielen	
(to) go to the gym	ins Fitness-Studio gehen	
(to) teach English (to) learn English (to) study English	Englisch unterrichten Englisch lernen Englisch üben, lernen	
(to) use a computer	einen Computer benutzen	
(to) speak English/German	Englisch/Deutsch sprechen	
I like PE (too). I don't like history.	Ich mag (auch) Sport. Ich mag Geschichte nicht.	

School subjects (Schulfächer)
art Kunst • **English** Englisch • **German** Deutsch •
geography Geografie • **history** Geschichte • **ICT** Informatik •
maths Mathe • **music** Musik • **PE** Sport • **science** Nawi

It's Tuesday.	Es ist Dienstag.	

The days of the week (Die Wochentage)
Monday Montag • **Tuesday** Dienstag •
Wednesday Mittwoch • **Thursday** Donnerstag •
Friday Freitag • **Saturday** Samstag • **Sunday** Sonntag

on Wednesdays on Wednesday	mittwochs, jeden Mittwoch am Mittwoch	
at the weekend	am Wochenende	

English	German	My notes
after school	nach der Schule	
What do we do every Tuesday?	Was machen wir jeden Dienstag?	
never	nie	
sometimes	manchmal	
usually	meistens, normalerweise	
every day	jeden Tag	
always	immer	
School starts at 8 o'clock. School finishes at 3:15.	Die Schule beginnt um 8 Uhr. Die Schule ist um 3:15 zu Ende.	

The numbers from 20 to 99 (Die Zahlen von 20 bis 99)
20 twenty, 21 twenty-one, 22 twenty-two, 23 twenty-three, …
29 twenty-nine

30 thirty	40 forty	50 fifty	60 sixty
70 seventy	80 eighty	90 ninety	→ Numbers, p. 111

from 9 **to** 11 o'clock	von 9 bis 11	

What's the time?   Wieviel Uhr ist es?
It's …   Es ist …
quarter past ten   Viertel nach zehn (*10:15 oder 22:15*)
half past ten   halb elf (*10:30 oder 22:30*)
quarter to eleven   Viertel vor elf (*10:45 oder 22:45*)

School things:	**Schulsachen:**	
pencil	der Bleistift	
pen	der Kugelschreiber, der Stift, der Füller	
timetable	der Stundenplan	
exercise book	das Übungsheft	
computer	der Computer	
test	der Test	
lesson	die Unterrichtsstunde	
break	die Pause	
(to) wear a school uniform / your own clothes	eine Schuluniform / die eigene Kleidung tragen	
(to) get a mark	eine Note bekommen	

Family:
mother
father
brother
sister
cousin
best friend

→ My Words, pp. 40–41

◯ Yero, Olga's father and Yero's mother

◯ Olga, Mr Chan and Olga's cousin

◯ Mo, Mo's best friend and a classmate

1 A class party with family and friends

a 🔊32–34 📑 Listen to and read the dialogues 1–3.

b 📑 ✏️ Find the groups of people on page 30 and number them (1–3).

1

Mr Chan:	Good morning, I'm Olga's teacher. And who are you? Are you Olga's mother?
Dina:	No, I'm Olga's cousin Dina. Olga's father, Mr Orlow, is the man over there.
Olga:	Look, Mr Chan. This is my mother. And this is my big sister. They live in Russia.

2

Nico:	Where do you sit, Mo?
Mo:	I usually sit here.
Nico:	Cool. What do you usually do in your English lessons?
Mo:	We talk in English, we watch videos …
Classmate:	And we make videos.
Nico:	Videos? That's so cool! I'm so bored at my school. Why can't we make videos?

3

Yero:	Do you like our chillout zone, Mr Orlow? The blue sofa is old and the white shelves are new.
Mr Orlow:	Yes, I do.
Yero:	And you, Mum? What do you like most about our chillout zone?
Mrs Touré:	I like the colours most. And I like your birthday calendar.

c ✂️ 📑 Match the questions to the answers. Check your answers in dialogues 1–3.

1 Where does Olga's mum live?

2 Who is Nico?

3 Why is Nico bored at his school?

4 Does Mr Orlow like the chillout zone?

5 What does Mrs Touré like most about the chillout zone?

A He is Mo's best friend.

B Yes, he does.

C She likes the colours most.

D She lives in Russia.

E Because they don't make videos at his school.

---

party
Who are you?
man
big sister
(to) live (in)

Where do you sit?
Why can't we make videos?
(to) be bored
(to) talk (to sb./ about sth.)
(to) make
(to) watch
cool
Do you like our chillout zone?
Yes, I do.
No, I don't.
birthday calendar
sofa
shelf, pl shelves
new
What do you like most about …?
because

English and German

when?	wann?
what?	was?
where?	wo?
why?	warum?
who?	wer?

→ My Words, pp. 40–41

1 The simple present: questions and short answers

a 🔊35 📖 Listen and read.

Olga: Do you like the new furniture, Mr Chan?
Mr Chan: Yes, I do. And do you like it, Olga?
Olga: Yes, I do. What about Jill? Does she like it?
Mr Chan: Yes, she does. And Mo and Yero?
Do they like the new furniture?
Olga: Yero does, but Mo doesn't.
He doesn't like the colours.
Mr Chan: That's too bad!

b 📖 ✏ Read the boxes. Then mark in the dialogue in 1a: questions with *do* and short answers.

Do	I you we you they	like the furniture? make videos?
Does	he/she/it Mo	like the colours?

Yes,	I/you we/you/they	do.
No,		don't.
Yes,	he/she/it	does.
No,		doesn't.

c ✏ Write five questions about your school in your exercise book.

Do you like	the birthday calendar • break time • the shelves • the sofa • the tables • the chillout zone • ...	in our classroom? at our school?

d 👥💬✏ Ask a partner. Write down his or her answers in your exercise book.

Questions	My partner's answers
Do you like the shelves in our classroom?	Yes, I do.

2 The simple present: questions and short answers with *be* and *can*

📖 ✏ Read the box. Write questions and answer them in your exercise book.

⚠ Never use *do* with *be* or *can*: Are you Olga's mother? Can you see Olga's father?	No, I'm not. Yes, I can.

→ Module 1, pp. 6–7 (be); Module 2, p. 19 (can)

1 nice | your classmates | Are | ?
2 your classroom | new | Is | ?
3 watch | Can | videos | in class | you | ?
4 Can | your smartphones | use | you | in class | ?

1. Are your classmates nice? – Yes, they are.

3 The simple present: questions with question words

a 🔊36 📖 Listen and read.

Let me ask you some questions, Yero. **When** is your birthday?

Who is your favourite celebrity?

What do you do on Saturdays?

When are you bored?

Why do you like our chillout zone?

It's in July.

My favourite celebrity is the footballer Thierno Bah.

I usually go to the gym.

I'm bored at the weekend sometimes.

Because I like the chairs. I usually sit there at break time.

b 📖 ✏ Find the question words in 3a and mark them in different colours:
what, when, why, who

c 📖 ✏ Read the boxes. Write the questions from 3a in the table.

Questions with question words:
What do I like best?
Where do you go?
When does school start?
Why does he like the chillout zone?

Question words with *be* and *can*:
Who are you?
When is your birthday?
What can you see?
When are you bored?

Questions with question words + *do*	Questions with question words only
What do you	When are you

d 👥 💬 ✏ Choose three questions from 3a (you can change the green words).
Ask a classmate or a friend. Write the questions and answers in your exercise book.

Questions	My partner's answers
What do you do on Sundays?	I usually play basketball on Saturdays.

Family:
mother – mum
father – dad
brother
sister
grandmother – grandma
grandfather – grandpa
aunt
uncle
cousin
good friend

my
your
his
her
our
their

1 Family and good friends

a 🔊 37 ✏️ Look at Olga's family photos. Listen and write the family words.

This is my family.
Anne and Jan are
good friends.
They're like family.

1 *mother*	5 _____	9 _____
2 _____	6 _____	10 _____
3 _____	7 _____	11 _____
4 _____	8 _____	

English and German
Jill**'s** family photo
Jill**s** Familienfoto

partner
half-brother / half-sister
great
happy
little brother ↔
big brother

b 🔊 38 ✏️ Look at Jill's family photo. Listen and number.

This is me
and my family.

c 🔊 39 ✏️ Listen and complete the text.

> aunt's • cool • dad's • little • great • happy • has •
> He's • ~~mum's~~ • new partner • She's

Short and long forms
He**'s** five. = He **is** five.
She**'s** cool. = She **is** cool.

My *mum's* name is Mary. She has a _____, Henry. My _____

half-brother's name is Oliver. _____ five. He always looks _____.

My _____ name is Jane. _____ really _____. She _____ red hair.

My _____ name is Pete. He's _____! He sends me funny messages every day.

d ✏️ Write in your exercise book about a friend or a family member.

My sister's name is ... She's ...

→ My Words, pp. 40–41

2 The birthday calendar

a 🔊40 📖 Listen to and read the months in the margin.

b 🔊41 ✏️ Listen to the dialogue. Write about Mo, Olga and Yero's birthdays.

> Let's have a look at our birthday calendar. My birthday is in June. It's on the twentieth of June. When's your birthday?

HAPPY BIRTHDAY!

5th January	Mo
8th February	Selina
12th April	Jill
20th June	Mr Chan
31st July	Yero
3rd August	Olga
11th August	Nino

Jill: *It's in April. It's on the twelfth of April.*

Mo: _____

Olga: _____

Yero: _____

c ✏️ Write about your birthday in your exercise book.
Check online about celebrities with the same birthday.

My birthday is in ... It's on the ... .
These celebrities have the same birthday: ...

3 A birthday invitation

a 📖 ✂️ Read. Then match the questions to the answers.

INVITATION – It's my birthday.

Date: Saturday, 5th July
Place: at the youth club

Time: from 4.00 to 8.30 pm
See you at my party!
Yero

---

1 What's this?

2 Why does Yero celebrate?

3 Where does he celebrate?

4 When is the party?

A Because it's his birthday.

B It's on Saturday, the fifth of July.

C It's a birthday invitation.

D He celebrates at the youth club.

4 Thinking about languages

a ✏️💬 Write the months in your language(s) and say them.

b 👥💬 Compare with your classmates.

When's your birthday?
It's in June.
It's on the twelfth of June.

Months:
January
February
March
April
May
June
July
August
September
October
November
December

Ordinal numbers:
1st first
2nd second
3rd third
4th fourth
5th fifth
6th sixth
7th seventh
8th eighth
9th ninth
10th tenth
11th eleventh
12th twelfth
13th thirteenth
14th fourteenth
15th fifteenth
16th sixteenth
17th seventeenth
18th eighteenth
19th nineteenth
20th twentieth
21st twenty-first
...

(to) celebrate

→ Numbers, p. 111
→ My Words, pp. 40–41

Furniture:
chair
shelf, *pl* shelves
sofa
table
rug
cushion

5 Furniture

a 🔊42 ✏️ Listen and look. Write down the furniture words 1–6.

1 _____	4 _____
2 _____	5 _____
3 _____	6 _____

> a chair • a shelf •
> a sofa • a table •
> a rug • a cushion

b ✏️ Look at the picture in 3a again. Complete the text with the singular or plural of the furniture words.

I really like the chillout zone in our classroom. There's a big yellow _____ in the middle. There are also _____ in different colours – purple, blue and orange. There's an old blue _____ on the left.

There are big green _____ on the sofa. Here we can sit and read or relax. There are white _____ for our books. And there are small, old _____ on the left and right.

Singular and plural
There**'s (is)** a rug.
There **are** five chairs.

on the left
on the right
in the middle

small

c 🔊43 📖 Listen and check.
d ✏️ Draw your dream chillout zone and write about it.
You can use the ideas from the box.

→ Module 1, p. 15
(colours)

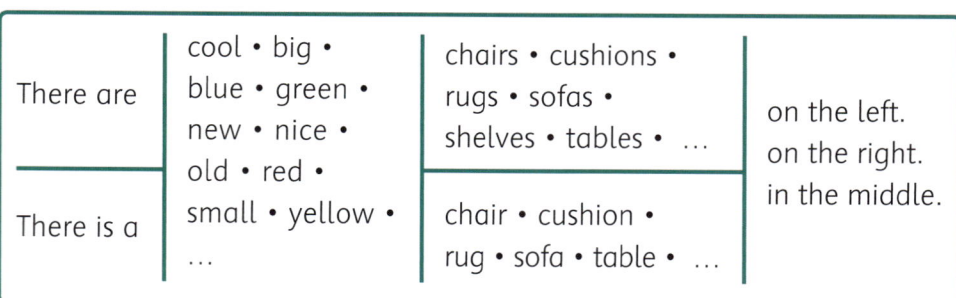

→ My Words, pp. 40–41

This is my dream chillout zone.
There are cool big cushions on the left …

6 An interview

a ✏ Find out interesting things about people in your class or at your school. Make a table and write down questions.

TIP: Change the green words in the questions:
Who is your favourite celebrity?
→ Who is your favourite teacher?

	Me	Partner 1	Partner 2
1 Who is your favourite celebrity?			
2 What is your favourite music?			
3 When are you bored?			
4 Where are you from?			
5 Do you like school?			
6 Do you have brothers or sisters?			
7 …			

teacher • …

month • school subject • …

happy • …

are your parents • is your best friend • …

English • maths • pizza • …

cousins • aunts • uncles • …

(to) be interested in sth.

TIP: You can look up more words in an online dictionary or in the online English-German dictionary for this workbook.

b 👥 💬 Ask people in a friendly way.

Excuse me, can I ask you some questions?

Yes, sure.

No, thanks.

c ✏ Write your partners' answers in your table.

Questions	Me	Partner 1: Nahla
1. Who is your favourite celebrity?	Lucas Torreira	Jimin from BTS
2. What is your favourite music?	pop	

Reporting
Nahla: "My favourite celebrity is Jimin."
→ Nahla's/Her favourite celebrity is Jimin.

Theo: "My favourite music is rap."
→ Theo's/His favourite music is rap.

d ✏ 💬 Write down people's answers in full sentences. Report to the class.

1. My favourite celebrity is Lucas Torreira. Nahla's favourite celebrity is Jimin from BTS.
2. My favourite music is pop. Her favourite music is …

→ My Words, pp. 40–41

TIP: You don't need to understand every word.

1 Understanding new words

a ▤▤ Look at the brochures.

GREEN LIFE

Great ideas for birthday presents.
Make teens happy with these
birthday presents.

~~~~~~~~~~~~~~~~~~~~~~~~~~~

**All our ideas are friendly
to the environment!**

T-shirts
water bottles
wristbands
chocolate

MODERN SCHOOL

Bored with grey chairs and tables in
your classroom?
Check out our high-top tables and
stools! Try our colourful pouffes.

Work at our high-top tables.
You can stand or sit on stools. And
during break time relax on pouffes.

pouffes
stools

TIP: How to understand new words:
1. Look at the pictures.
2. Do you understand a part of the word?
3. Think about other languages.
4. Check the context of the word.

b ▤▤ Try to understand the marked words in the brochures.
Use these tips:

1. Look at the pictures.

water bottles

2. You know one part of the word.
Can you guess the other part?

friendly: friend + ly

3. Think about words in
other languages.

chocolate:
Schokolade, czekolada, cioccolata,
çikolata, chocolat, …

4. Check the context of the word.
Can you guess the other part?

Work at our high-top tables.
You can stand or sit on stools.

c ✎ Write the marked words from 1a in English, German
and your language(s) in your exercise book.

English	German	Your language(s)
water bottle	(die) Wasserflasche	
…		

d ▤▤ Check the words in a dictionary.

Checkpoint

1 ✎ Write the questions and answer them.

1 you | school | ~~Do~~ | like | ?

Do

2 two languages | speak | your family | Does | ?

3 your friends | Do | videos | watch | ?

2 ✎ Complete the questions with *why*, *what*, *when* and *where*.

1 _____ is this?   This is an invitation.

2 _____ is the party?   The party is at school.

3 _____ is the party?   It's next Friday.

4 _____ do we celebrate? Because we have a new classroom.

INVITATION
to our class party
on Friday, 5th May

3 🔊44 ✎ Listen and write down the family words.

1 _____ **6** _____

2 _____ **7** _____

3 _____ **8** _____

4 _____ **9** _____

5 _____

4 ✎ Complete the sentences.

When is your birthday?   My birthday is in _____.

                         My birthday is on _____.

5 ✎ Write down five or more furniture words.

_____

_____

thirty-nine   39

English	German	My notes
Family and friends:	**Familie und Freunde:**	
mother – mum father – dad	die Mutter – Mama der Vater – Papa	
brother sister	der Bruder die Schwester	
half-brother half-sister	der Halbbruder die Halbschwester	
grandmother – grandma grandfather – grandpa	die Großmutter – Oma der Großvater – Opa	
aunt uncle	die Tante der Onkel	
cousin	der Cousin / die Cousine	
partner	der Partner / die Partnerin	
best friend	der beste Freund / die beste Freundin	
man, *pl* men woman, *pl* women	der Mann, *Pl.* die Männer die Frau, *Pl.* die Frauen	

my, your, his, her, our, their
my mother meine Mutter • **your father** dein/euer Vater •
his uncle sein Onkel • **her brother** ihr Bruder •
our aunt unsere Tante • **their cousin** ihre Cousine

because	weil	
party	die Party	

Describing people/things (Personen/Dinge beschreiben)
bored gelangweilt • **cool** cool, toll • **good** gut •
great großartig, toll • **nice** nett, hübsch •
big *(age, size)* groß • **little** *(age, size)* klein •
small *(size)* klein • **happy** glücklich, froh • **new** neu • **old** alt

(to) live (in)	leben, wohnen (in)	
(to) talk (to sb. / about sth.)	reden (mit jm. / über etwas)	
(to) watch (a video)	(ein Video) anschauen	
(to) make	machen	
(to) celebrate	feiern	
on the left / on the right in the middle	links / rechts in der Mitte	

My Words

English	German	My notes
Who are you?	Wer bist du? / Wer sind Sie?	
Who is your favourite celebrity?	Wer ist deine liebste Prominente / dein liebster Prominenter?	
What do you like most about …?	Was magst du am meisten an …? / Was mögen Sie …?	
Where do you sit?	Wo sitzt du? / Wo sitzen Sie?	
When are you bored?	Wann ist dir/Ihnen langweilig?	
Why can't we make videos?	Warum können wir keine Videos machen?	
Do you like …? Yes, I do. / No, I don't.	Magst du …? / Mögen Sie …? Ja. / Nein.	

Months (Monate)
January Januar • **February** Februar • **March** März •
April April • **May** Mai• **June** Juni • **July** Juli • **August** August •
September September • **October** Oktober •
November November • **December** Dezember

English	German	My notes
When's your birthday? My birthday is **in May**. My birthday is **on the twelfth of June**.	Wann hast du Geburtstag? Ich habe im Mai Geburtstag. Ich habe am zwölften Juni Geburtstag.	
birthday calendar	der Geburtstagskalender	

Ordinal numbers (Ordinalzahlen)
1st first der/die/das erste, **2nd second**, **3rd third**, **4th fourth**,
5th fifth, **6th sixth**, **7th seventh**, **8th eighth**, **9th ninth**,
10th tenth, **11th eleventh**, **12th twelfth**, **20th twentieth**,
21st twenty-first, … → Numbers, p. 111

Furniture:	**Möbel:**	
chair	der Stuhl	
table	der Tisch	
shelf, *pl* shelves	das Regal, *Pl.* die Regale	
rug	der Teppich	
sofa	das Sofa	
cushion	das Kissen	

4 Free-time activities

Where were you
last weekend?

I was at the youth club.

I was at home.

What did you do?

I played football.

I watched football on TV.

It was fun/great/
very exciting.

Was it fun?

Yes, it was.

No, it wasn't.

at the youth club

(to) practise

(to) dance

(to) stop

(to) cheer

(to) play football

(to) win a match,
simple past: won

(to) watch (TV, a film)

(to) have a cold,
simple past: had

(to) do sport,
simple past: did

(to) be at home,
simple past: was, were

(to) go to bed early,
simple past: went

but
then
because
lots of

→ My Words, pp. 54–55

1 What did they do last weekend?

a 🔊45 📖 Look at page 42. Listen to and read the dialogue.

b ⚃ Who did what? Match the sentences to the pictures.

1 She practised with her drama group.

2 He watched football on TV.

3 He danced with his friends.

4 He played football.

Picture A

Picture B

Picture C

Picture D

c 📖 ✓ How was it? Read again. Tick the right answers.

	Yes, it was.	No, it wasn't.
1 Olga's weekend was exciting.	☐	✔
2 Mo's weekend was great.	☐	☐
3 Mr Chan's weekend was fun.	☐	☐
4 Yero's weekend was OK.	☐	☐

2 More free-time activities

a 🔊46 💬 Look at the pictures and listen. Listen again and repeat.

play video games

take photos

listen to music

visit your grandma

meet friends

chat with friends

b ✏ What did they do yesterday?
Complete the sentences.

chatted • listened • met • played • took • visited

1 Basar and Jo *played* video games.

2 Mia _____ photos in the park.

3 Cero _____ to music.

4 Sandra _____ her grandma.

5 Milan _____ his friends in a cafe.

6 Sue _____ with her best friend.

c 🔊47 📖 Listen and check.

Free-time activities:
(to) visit your grandma
(to) play video games
(to) take photos (of)
(to) listen to music
(to) meet friends
(to) chat with friends

yesterday
in the park

→ My Words, pp. 54–55

4   Free-time activities

1 The simple past: positive statements

a 📖 ✏️ Read about the simple past with regular verbs.
Then complete the sentences with the simple past of the verbs.

I	
You	practised.
He/She/It	danced.
We	played.
You	
They	

You form the simple past of regular verbs with -ed.

⚠ Be careful with the spelling of these verbs:
practise, dance: practised, danced
chat, stop: chatted, stopped
study: studied   (but: play – played)

I studied for the English test yesterday.
Last weekend we visited my grandmother.
I played football with my friends on Sunday.

You use the simple past to say what you did
or what happened in the past.
Signal words: yesterday, last week, last year,
on Monday, at 8 o'clock, …

1 I _____ (play) video games yesterday.

2 Mo _____ (chat) with Yero last Friday.

3 They _____ (watch) TV yesterday.

4 Olga _____ (study) last weekend.

5 School _____ (start) at 8 o'clock.

6 I _____ (dance) on Saturday.

b ✏️ ✏️ Mark the signal words in sentences 1–6.
c 📖 ✏️ Read about the simple past with irregular verbs. Write the simple past forms in the table.
(You can find them on pages 42–43.)

I	
You	had a cold.
He/She/It	was at home.
We	met friends.
You	
They	

There is no rule for the simple past of
irregular verbs. You need to learn them.

→ Irregular verbs, pp. 108–109

irregular verb	simple past
be	was, were
have	
meet	
take	
win	

d ✏️ Complete the text with the simple past of the regular verbs and irregular verbs.

Jill _____ (have) a nice weekend. On Saturday morning she _____ (chat) online with her dad.

They _____ (talk) about their favourite rugby teams. Then she _____ (watched) a rugby

game at the stadium. A team from her club _____ (play) – and they _____ (win).

She _____ (take) lots of photos. She _____ (show) her photos to the players and

they _____ (like) them. Jill _____ (be) very happy!

3 The simple past: negative statements

a 📖 ✏️ Read the box. Then complete the sentences with the negative forms of the verbs in the box.

I You He/She/It We You They	didn't (= did not)	practise. dance. go.

You make negative statements in the simple past with didn't and the infinitive of the verb:
He didn't watch TV.

⚠ not: He didn't watched TV

1 Yero _____ TV yesterday.

2 Mr Chan _____ sport at the weekend.

3 Olga _____ with her cousin on Saturday.

4 Mo _____ video games on Sunday.

chat • do • met • play • watch

b 📖 ✏️ At the weekend Yero had a list of things to do. Read Yero's list. Write what he <u>didn't</u> do.

1 *Yero didn't do his maths homework.*
_____

2 *He* _____

3 _____

4 _____

5 _____

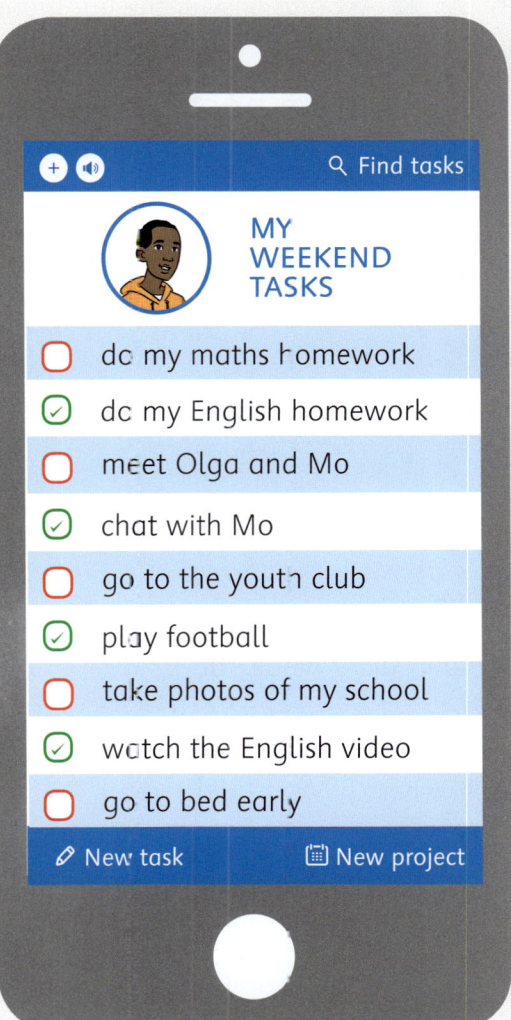

c 📖 ✏️ Read again. Write what Yero <u>did</u>. Use positive sentences.(Look at page 44 for help.)

1 *Yero did his* _____

2 *He* _____

3 _____

4 _____

d ✏️ What did you do last weekend?
Write three sentences in your exercise book.

I visited my aunt, ...

e 👥 💬 Compare your sentences with a partner.

3 The simple past: questions and short answers

a 📖 ✏ Read the boxes. Write four or more questions in your exercise book and answer them.

Did	I you he/she/it we you they	watch a film? stop? meet friends?		Yes,	I/you he/she/it we/you/they	did.
				No,	I/you he/she/it we/you/they	didn't.

Did	you you and your friends	go to the youth club • play football / video games • do sport • meet friends • listen to music • watch a film • …	last weekend? yesterday?

Did you go to the youth club last weekend? – No, I didn't.

b 👥 💬 Ask and answer the questions with a partner.

4 The simple past: questions with question words

a 📖 ✏ Read the boxes. Then write the questions and answer them.

What Where When	did	I you he/she/it we you they	watch? meet? stop?

Questions
How did you like it?
What did you watch?

The verb forms *like*, *watch* are infinitives.

Answers
I liked it very much.
We watched a film.

The verb forms *liked*, *watched* are simple past forms.

1 Where | yesterday | you | did | go | ?

Where did _____   *I went* _____

2 you | did | What | do | ?

_____   *I/We* _____

3 like best | What | did | you | ?

_____   _____

4 to bed | When | go | you | did | ?

_____   *I* _____

5 The simple past of the verb *be*: positive and negative statements

a 📖 ✏️ Read the boxes. Then mark the right words in the sentences:
was, *were*, *wasn't* or *weren't*.

I He/She/It Yero/Jill	was	at home.	
You We They	were	at home.	

I He/She/It Yero/Jill	wasn't	at home.	
You We They	weren't	at home.	

1 Mo's dance contest **was / were** at the park.

2 Mr Chan **wasn't / weren't** at the theatre.

3 Yero's friends **was / were** at the stadium.

4 The students **wasn't / weren't** at school

5 Olga **was / were** at the youth club.

6 Mr Chan and his friend **was / were** at home.

6 The simple past of the verb *be*: questions and short answers

a 📖 ✍️ Read the boxes. Then match the questions to the answers.

Was	I He/She/It Yero/Jill	at home?	Yes, No,	I/you he/she/it	was. wasn't.	
Were	You We They	at home?	Yes, No,	we/you/they	were. weren't.	

Questions with question words:
How was your weekend?
Who was there?
When were you at home?

1 How was your weekend?

2 Where were you?

3 Who was with you?

4 Why did you go there?

5 Was the film good?

6 When were you home again?

7 Was Dina with you?

A My cousin Dina was with me.

B Because they showed a film about Russia.

C It was very nice.

D No, she wasn't.

E I was at the youth club.

F I was at home at 10 o'clock.

G Yes, it was!

Hi, Olga. How was your weekend?

It was very nice.

b 🔊48 📖 Listen to the dialogue and check your answers.

TIP: How to understand new words:
1. Look at the pictures.
2. Think about other languages.
3. Do you understand parts of the word?
4. Check the context of the word.

→ Module 3, p.38 (Understanding new words)

(very) popular
(to) do exercises
training
first
(to) love sth./sb.

1 Jill's weekend blog

a 🔊49 📖 Listen to and read Jill's blog.

JILL'S WEEKEND BLOG

🏠 Home   💬 🔍

Last weekend I was at a rugby camp. In Britain rugby is a very popular team sport. In Germany rugby isn't very popular. But I was lucky: there's a rugby club in my German hometown!
In a rugby game there are two teams of 15 players. They play with an oval ball and two H-shaped goals. The team that scores more points wins the game. Read more about rugby

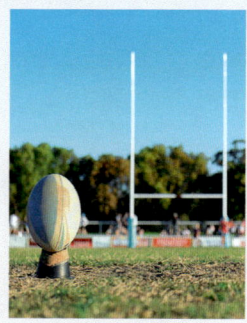

5th May
Training started at 5 pm. First we did special exercises.
Read more about our exercises

6th May
We learned lots of new rugby skills. It was very hard. But we had lots of fun too!
Read more about rugby skills

7th May
The girls were so great! I just love my team!
Read more about my rugby team

🏷 rugby, fun, sports, camp, training

like   💬 comment   ↗ share   0 comments

b 📖 ⚄ Read again. Match the dates to the titles.

1 5th May   **A** What we learned

2 6th May   **B** My team was great!

3 7th May   **C** A good start

c 📖 ✏ Read again. Tick the right answers.

1 Jill was at a …   ◯ rugby camp.   ◯ rugby match.

2 Rugby is very popular in …   ◯ Germany.   ◯ Britain.

3 Training started on …   ◯ 5th May.   ◯ 5th March.

4 The girls learned lots of …   ◯ new subjects.   ◯ new skills.

→ My Words, pp.54–55

2 Sports week at school

a 🔊50 📖 ✏ Who did what sport? Listen and read. Write letters:
M for Mo, *O* for Olga and *Y* for Yero.

Sports:
(to) play table tennis
(to) do exercises
(to) go skateboarding
(to) do kung fu
(to) play chess
(to) go swimming

do exercises

play chess

play table tennis

do kung fu

go skateboarding

go swimming

b ✏ Write positive sentences. Use the simple past of *do*, *play* and *go*.

1 *Olga did exercises and* _____

2 *Mo* _____

3 *Yero* _____

Positive and negative statements
Mo **played** chess.
Mo **didn't play** chess.

c ✏ What <u>didn't</u> they do? Write negative sentences.

1 *Olga didn't play chess, go swimming, do kung fu or play table tennis.*

2 *Mo* _____

_____

3 *Yero* _____

_____

English and German
I **listened** to music.
Ich **habe** Musik **gehört**.
Ich **hörte** Musik.

You **listened** to music.
Du **hast** Musik **gehört**.
Du **hörtest** Musik.

She **listened** to music.
Sie **hat** Musik **gehört**.
Sie **hörte** Musik.

3 Thinking about cultures

a 👥 💬 What sports are popular in your home country or in other countries? Talk to a partner.

b 📖 Choose one sport and find more information about it:
– How many players are there?
– Who wins the game?
– …

c 👥 💬 Tell your partner about your sport.

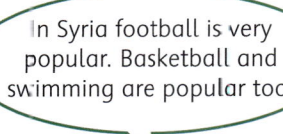
In Syria football is very popular. Basketball and swimming are popular too.

In Russia ice hockey and chess are very popular. But football is popular too.

→ My Words, pp. 54–55

4 Last week was different

a 📖 ✏ Read. Mark the right verb forms: simple present or simple past.

Last week Mr Chan **have / had** a cold. He
isn't / wasn't at school and so lots of things
are / were different. We usually **have / had** English
on Tuesdays and Thursdays. But last week we
don't have / didn't have English on Tuesday.
We **have / had** maths with Mrs Kern. Olga **is / was**
happy because she **likes / liked** maths. We often
watch / watched English videos with Mr Chan.
But Mrs Kern **doesn't watch / didn't watch** a video
with us. She **does / did** a maths test! On Thursday
we **have / had** English with Jill. It **is / was** really
cool! We **listen / listened** to music and we **make /
made** our own songs. Jill **records / recorded** our
songs so Mr Chan can listen to them.

b 🔊51 📖 Listen and check.

5 Mr Chan had a cold last week

a ✏ What <u>didn't</u> Mr Chan do last week? Look and write.

1 *He didn't go* _____ (not go swimming)

2 _____ (not play video games)

3 _____ (not go to school)

4 _____ (not do exercises)

b ✏ What didn't you do last week? Write three sentences or more
in your exercise book.

I didn't	play	football • table tennis • video games • …	last week.
	do	exercises • my homework • sport • …	
	go	swimming • to bed early • to school • …	

I didn't do exercises last week.

c 👥 💬 Compare your sentences with a partner.

---

different
so
(to) make,
simple past: made

**Simple present and
simple past**

Use the **simple present**
to say what usually,
always, never happens:
I **go**, you **play**,
he/she/it **likes**, …

→ Module 2, pp. 18–19

Use the **simple past** to
say what happened
yesterday, last week, …:
I **went**, you **played**,
he/she/it **liked**, …

→ My Words, pp. 54–55

6 Your blog post *A great day*

a ✎ Collect your ideas in this mind map. You can use ideas from the boxes.

TIP: Look up words in an online dictionary or in the English-German dictionary for this workbook.

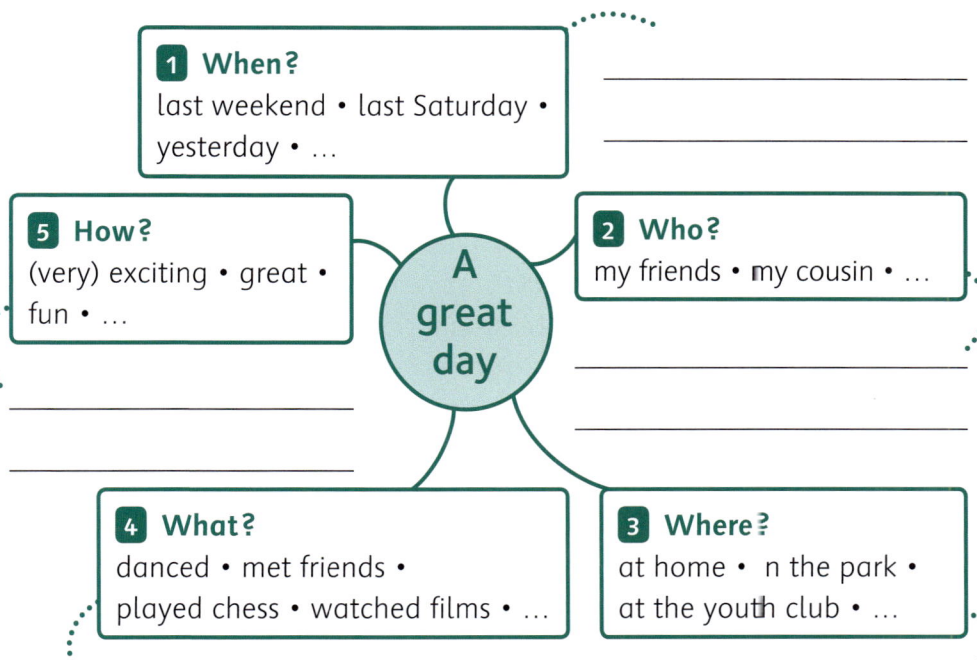

1 When?
last weekend • last Saturday • yesterday • …

_____

_____

5 How?
(very) exciting • great • fun • …

_____

_____

A great day

2 Who?
my friends • my cousin • …

_____

_____

4 What?
danced • met friends • played chess • watched films • …

_____

_____

3 Where?
at home • in the park • at the youth club • …

_____

_____

b ✎ Write your blog post. Use your ideas from 6a.

```
• • •

posted by _____ on _____

1 _____ I had a great day!

2  I was with _____

3  We were _____

4  We _____

   _____

5  It was _____

👍 like     💬 comment     🔗 share
```

c 👥💬 Interview your partner about his or her great day. Ask these questions:

1 When was your great day?
2 Who was with you?
3 Where were you?

4 What did you do?
5 How was it?
6 …

d ✎ Write about your partner's day in your exercise book.

Last Sunday Ira had a great day. She was with …

Reporting
Sirin: "Last weekend I had a great day."
→ *Last weekend Sirin had a great day.*

→ My Words, pp. 54–55

Dear
Hello
Hi
Love
Best wishes

(to) have to,
simple past: had to

1 How to write better emails

a 📖 ✏️ Read Jill's emails. How can you start and finish an email?
Write the words from the box on the right line.

Start an email: _____

Finish an email: _____

> Best wishes •
> Dear • Hello •
> Hi • Love

● ● ●

Subject: An exciting week!
Hi Dad
How are you? How was your week? Last
week Mr Chan had a cold, so I had to teach
English and Mrs Kern taught the other subjects.
It was very exciting because on Thursday
I was alone with the class! First we listened to
music and talked about it. Then the kids
made their own songs. They were really good
and I think they liked my English lesson!
What did you do? Please write soon!
Love
Jill

● ● ●

Subject: Last week!
Dear Mr Chan
How are you?
Last week was special because we had
to manage without you. First the students
weren't happy because they like your
English lessons best. But then they were OK.
On Thursday we listened to some music
and then students made their own songs.
The students say hello to you.
Get well soon.
Best wishes
Jill Corothers

---

b 📖 ✏️ Find these words in the emails in 1a and mark them
with the right colour:

> **Time words:**
> last weekend, on Thursday,
> first, then

> **Linking words:**
> and, but, because, so

TIP: Use time words
and linking words
to make your text
interesting.

time words:
last weekend, on
Monday/…, first,
then, …

linking words:
and, but, so,
because, …

TIP: You can use ideas
from p. 51.

c ✏️ Write an email to a friend or a teacher about last weekend.
(Write on the computer or in your exercise book.)

1 Write the subject on the subject line.

2 Start the email with *Dear* or *Hello.*

3 Ask questions.

4 Write about what you did last
weekend. Use the simple past.

5 Use time words and linking words.

6 Finish the email with *Best wishes*
or *Love* and your name.

d 👥📖 Check your text with your
teacher or a partner.

● ● ●

Subject: … **1**

Dear/Hello … **2**

How are you? **3**

Last weekend I went … **4**

First … and then … because … **5**

How was your weekend? **3**

Love/Best wishes … **6**

→ My Words, pp. 54–55

1 ✎ Write the sports and activities under the pictures.

go _____   _____   _____   _____

2 ✎ Complete the dialogue with *was, were, wasn't, weren't*.

Taio: Hi, Ava! How _____ (1) your weekend?

Ava: It _____ (2) OK, thanks. My best friend and I _____ (3) at a concert.

Taio: _____ (4) it fun?

Ava: No, it _____ (5). I _____ (6) there very early, but my friend _____ (7). Then my friend _____ (8) there, but the band _____ (9)! The concert started two hours late.

Taio: _____ (10) the music good?

Ava: It _____ (11) OK. It _____ (12) my favourite style of music.

3 ✎ Complete the text with the regular and irregular simple past forms.

Yesterday Yero and Mo _____ (go) to the stadium because their favourite football team _____ (play). The match _____ (be) very exciting. Their team _____ (win) 2:0. Yero and Mo _____ (cheer) and _____ (take) lots of photos. Later they _____ (watch) the best scenes on their smartphones and _____ (talk) about football for hours.

4 ✎ Mark the right words.

• • •

Dear/Hi Mrs Kern
Thank you for your help with my English lesson **next/last** week.
Your tips were very useful for me. **Then/First** I played English raps
but/because the students like music. **Yesterday/Then** the students
worked in groups **and/but** made songs.

Love/Best wishes
Jillian Corothers

English	German	My notes
What did you do last weekend?	Was hast du letztes Wochenende gemacht?/ Was haben Sie …?	
How was your weekend?	Wie war dein/Ihr Wochenende?	
Where were you?	Wo warst du?/ Wo waren Sie?	
Was it fun? Yes, it was./No, it wasn't.	Hat es Spaß gemacht? Ja./Nein.	

It was …/It's … (Es war …/Es ist …)
different anders(artig) • **exciting** aufregend, spannend • **great** großartig, toll • **OK** OK • **(very) popular** (sehr) beliebt • **It was fun.** Es hat Spaß gemacht.

English	German	My notes
training	das Training	
lots of sport/things/…	viel Sport/viele Dinge/…	
(to) practise	üben	
(to) love sth./sb.	etwas/jn. lieben	
(to) stop	aufhören	
(to) cheer	jubeln	
(to) watch a film	einen Film schauen	
(to) win a match	ein Match/ein Spiel gewinnen	
(to) have a cold	eine Erkältung haben	
(to) have to do sth.	etwas tun müssen	
(to) go to bed early	früh ins Bett gehen	

Irregular simple past forms

be	was/were	sein: war, ist gewesen
do	did	tun: tat, hat getan
go	went	gehen: ging, ist gegangen
have	had	haben: hatte, hat gehabt
make	made	machen: machte, hat gemacht
meet	met	treffen: traf, hat getroffen
take	took	nehmen: nahm, hat genommen
win	won	gewinnen: gewann, hat gewonnen

→ Irregular verbs, pp. 108–109

English	German	My notes
at the youth club	im Jugendzentrum	
at home	zu Hause	
in the park	im Park	

Linking words (Konjunktionen, Verbindungswörter)
and und • **because** weil • **but** aber • **so** also, daher
Time words (Zeitadverbien)
first zuerst • **then** dann • **yesterday** gestern • **last week** letzte
Woche • **last weekend** letztes Wochenende

Sports and other free-time activities:	**Sport und andere Freizeitaktivitäten:**	
(to) dance	tanzen	
(to) play football	Fußball spielen	
(to) play table tennis	Tischtennis spielen	
(to) play chess	Schach spielen	
(to) play video games	Videospiele spielen	
(to) do sport	Sport machen	
(to) go swimming	schwimmen gehen	
(to) go skateboarding	Skateboard fahren	
(to) do kung fu	Kung Fu machen	
(to) do exercises	Übungen/Gymnastik machen	
(to) visit your grandma	die Oma besuchen	
(to) take photos (of)	Fotos machen (von)	
(to) listen to music	Musik hören	
(to) meet friends	Freunde treffen	
(to) chat with friends	mit Freunden chatten (*per Internet*); reden, plaudern	

Writing emails and letters (E-Mails und Briefe schreiben)
Dear ... Liebe(r) ... • **Hi** ... Hi ... • **Hello** ... Hallo ... • **Best
wishes** Viele Grüße • **Love** Alles Liebe

5 Getting around town

What are you doing?

I'm lying under my favourite tree in the park.

Are you having fun?

No, I'm not. / Yes, I am.

at the moment

(right) now

today

Getting around town:

(to) sit at the bus stop

(to) wait for the bus

(to) go to the park / the cinema

(to) look for a bus ticket (in a rucksack)

(to) help sb.

(to) come

(to) stand in the queue

(to) buy snacks

O Hi guys! I'm lying under my favourite tree in the park. But I'm bored! What are you doing at the moment? Are you having fun?

No, I'm not! I'm in the park with my little sister. She's playing with a girl. And I'm looking for my bus ticket!

Not again! Where are you looking for your bus ticket today?

I'm looking for it in my rucksack right now.

I can help you, Yero. I'm sitting at the bus stop. I'm waiting for the bus to the park.

Sorry, I'm not going to the park. I'm going to the cinema with Nico. Good luck, Yero!

Yeah, good luck, Yero! I'm standing in the queue at the snack bar. I'm buying snacks.

→ My Words, pp. 66–67

1 I'm looking for my bus ticket!

a 🔊52 🗐 Look at page 56. Listen and read.

b 🗐 ✏ Read page 56 again and look at the pictures. Write *O* for Olga, *M* for Mo, *Y* for Yero, *D* for Dina and *N* for Nico.

c 🗐 ✂ What are they doing? Match the pictures to the sentences.

I'm going to the cinema with Nico.	I'm looking for my bus ticket.	I'm waiting for the bus to the park.	I'm lying under my favourite tree in the park.

2 What are they doing?

a 🔊53 ✏ Look and listen. Number the sentences (1–6).

 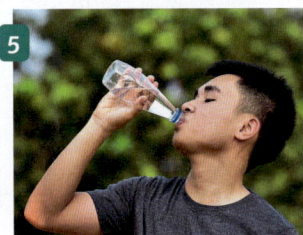 

(to) get ready for school
(to) drink water
(to) eat a sandwich
(to) read a book
(to) talk to each other

○ Leo is drinking water.

○ Sam is reading a book.

① Max is chatting with a friend.

○ Gabrielle is eating a sandwich.

○ Lily is getting ready for school.

○ Pina and Greta are talking to each other.

b ✏ What are your classmates doing now?
Write four or more sentences in your exercise book.

Lisa and Jakob are getting ready for maths.
Hasan is eating a sandwich.

TIP: Change the green words in the sentences from 2a:
Gabrielle is eating a sandwich.
→ *Leo and Greta are eating a pizza.*

→ My Words, pp. 66–67

1 The present progressive: positive statements

a 🔲 ✏ Read the boxes. Then complete the sentences with the present progressive of the verbs.

I'm (= am)	
You're (= are)	waiting.
He/She/It's (= is)	listening.
We're	reading.
You're	
They're	

You form the present progressive with am, are, is and the -ing form of the verb.

⚠ Be careful with the spelling of these verbs:
come, write: coming, writing
chat, get, sit: chatting, getting, sitting
lie: lying

I'm listening to music at the moment.
I'm talking to my best friend now.
The people (in the picture) are talking to each other.

You use the present progressive to say what somebody is doing now. You also use it to say what people are doing in pictures.
signal words: now, at the moment, …

1 Yero *is* _____ (look for) his bus ticket.

2 Olga _____ (help) Yero.

3 The little girls _____ (sit) in the playground.

4 They _____ (play) at the moment.

5 Now Dina _____ (come) to the playground.

b 🔲 ✏ Find the signal words in sentences 1–5 and mark them.

2 The present progressive: negative statements

a 🔲 ✏ Read the box. Then complete the sentences with the present progressive of the verbs.

I'm not …	
You aren't …	
He/She/It isn't	waiting.
We aren't	listening.
You aren't	reading.
They aren't	

1 Yero's sister _____ (not look for) the bus ticket.

2 Mo and Nico _____ (not go) to the park.

3 Yero and Olga _____ (not talk).

4 Yero _____ (not have) fun today.

b ✏ Look at the picture in 1. Where is Yero's bus ticket? Write and tick.

The bus ticket _____ (lie) under ⬤ ◯ the rucksack.   ◯ the books.   ◯ the apple.

3 The present progressive: questions and short answers

a 🔊 54 ▤▤ Listen and read.

Dina: Hi, Yero. Are you still looking for your ticket?
Yero: Yes, I am.
Dina: Is your sister helping you?
Yero: No, she isn't. She's playing. But Olga is helping.
Dina: Where is she looking for your ticket?
Yero: In the playground.
Dina: Sorry … What are you saying?
Yero: She's looking for it in the … yippee!
Dina: Why are you cheering?
Yero: Olga has the bus ticket! It was under my sister's books.

b ▤▤ ✂ Read the dialogue again. Match the questions to the answers.

1 What is Olga doing?

2 Where is she looking for it?

3 Why is Yero cheering?

A She's looking for it in the playground.

B Because Olga has the bus ticket.

C She's looking for Yero's bus ticket.

c ▤▤ ✏ Read the boxes. Then mark in the dialogue in 3a:
questions with question words or without question words.

Am I			Yes,	I am.	**Questions with question words:**
Are you				we/you/they are.	Who is helping you?
Is he/she/it	helping?			he/she/it is.	What are you doing?
Are we	waiting?		No,	I'm not.	Where is she looking?
Are you				we/you/they aren't.	Why are you cheering?
Are they				he/she/it isn't.	

4 Present progressive or simple present?

a ▤▤ Read the box and sentences.

1 Olga usually **eats** one sandwich for lunch.
2 Now Olga **is eating** two sandwiches.
3 Yero usually **drinks** water.
4 Today Yero **is drinking** tea.

> Use the simple present to say what somebody usually does.   → Module 2, p. 18 (simple present)
>
> Use the present progressive to say what somebody is doing now or only today.

b ▤▤ ✏ Read the sentences again. Number the pictures (1–4).

 ①

Means of transport:
(to) walk
(to) go by …
bike
car
bus
train
scooter

1 Means of transport

🔊55 📑 ✏️ Listen and read. Number the pictures (1–6).

1 walk
2 go by bike / take your bike
3 go by car / take your car
4 go by train / take the train
5 go by bus / take the bus
6 go by scooter / take your scooter

2 How are they getting around today?

a ✏️ Look at the pictures. Complete the sentences with the simple present or the present progressive.

Simple present and present progressive

Mon	Tues	Wed	Fri	Sat	Sun
✓	✓	✓	✓		

Olga usually **goes** to school by bus.
→ usually + simple present

Mon	Tues	Wed	Fri	Sat	Sun
		✓			

Today she**'s going** by bike.
→ today/now + present progressive

1 Olga usually _goes_ (go) by bus. But today she _'s going_ (go) by bike.

2 Mr Chan usually _____ (take) the train.

   But today he's _____ (take) his car.

3 Yero and his sister usually _____ (walk) home.

   But today they _____ (go) by bus.

4 Mrs Kern usually _____ (go) by bike.

   But today she _____ (go) by scooter.

5 Mo usually _____ (walk). But today he _____ (take) his bike.

6 Jill and her friend usually _____ (go) by bike.

   But today they _____ (walk).

English and German
She**'s talking**.
Sie **spricht** gerade.

→ My Words, pp. 66–67

b ✏️ Mark the simple present and present progressive forms.

3 Places in town

a 🔊56 📇 💬 Listen and read. Listen again and repeat.

a bike shop

a hairdresser's

a supermarket

a shopping centre

a mobile phone shop

a cafe

Places in town:
bike shop
mobile phone shop
shopping centre
cafe
supermarket
hairdresser's

b ✏️ Look at the map and number the places (1–9).

- ⭕ a cafe
- ⭕ a bike shop
- ⭕ a bus stop
- ⭕ Jill's flat
- ⭕ a hairdresser's
- ⭕ a mobile phone shop
- ⭕ a park
- ⭕ a shopping centre
- ⭕ a supermarket

c 📇 🔊57 ✏️ Where are these places? Read the sentences and look at the map. Then listen and mark the right words.

1 Jill's flat is **near**/**in** the park.
2 The bike shop is **next to**/**behind** the mobile phone shop.
3 The cafe is **in**/**at** Wing Street.
4 The shopping centre is **to**/**on** New Road.
5 The bus stop is **at**/**in front of** the supermarket.
6 The hairdresser's is **next to**/**near** the cafe.

d 👥 💬 Choose a place on the map and say where it is.
Can your partner say what the place is?

A: It's on Old Road and next to a cafe.
B: Is it a supermarket?
A: That's right./Sorry, that's wrong.

English and German
Jill's flat
Jills Wohnung

in the street
on the road
in front of
near
next to
opposite

→ My Words, pp. 66–67

Asking and telling the way:

How can you get from … to …?

Go along the street.

Turn right.

Turn left.

The … is on the right/left.

4 Getting around Jill's hometown

a 🔊58 💬 Look and listen. Listen again and repeat.

Go along New Road.

Turn right into Old Street.

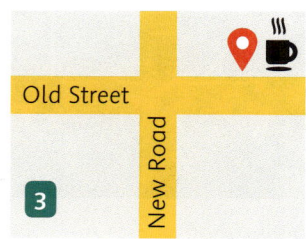
The cafe is on the left.

b 🔊59 📑 Listen and read. Can you see the bike shop on the map?

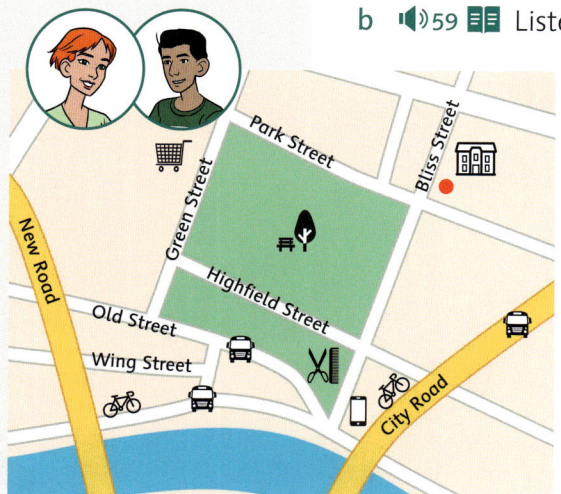

Jill: Look, Mo. This is a map of my hometown. My flat is in Bliss Street. That's near the park.

Mo: Cool. Let's see … I'm looking for a bike shop.

Jill: There's a bike shop on City Road.

Mo: How can you get from your flat to the bike shop?

Jill: Turn left and go along Bliss Street. Turn left into Highfield Street. Go along the street. Then turn right into City Road.

Mo: I can see the bike shop. It's on the right. And what about a supermarket and a hairdresser's?

c ✏ Describe the way from Jill's flat to the next supermarket (1) and to the hairdresser's (2) at the park.

1 Turn left and go _____ Bliss Street.

Turn _____ into Park Street and _____

into Green Street. The supermarket is on

the _____.

2 Turn _____ and go along Bliss Street.

Turn _____ into Highfield Street.

The hairdresser's is on the _____.

5 Thinking about languages

👥 ✋ ✏ Make a picture dictionary or a poster about places in your town. Write the places in English, German and your language(s).

supermarket
Supermarkt
супермáркет
سوبر ماركت

→ My Words, pp. 66–67

6 Helping a tourist in your town

a 📖 Read the text and look at the map.

Two classmates, a girl and a boy, are standing in front of your school.
A tourist asks them the way.

Excuse me, please. How can I get to *Hornweg* 4?

b 🔊60 ✏️ Listen to the dialogue. Who is right? Tick.

⭕ the girl   ⭕ the boy   ⭕ the girl and the boy   ⭕ no one

c 👥 ✏️ 💬 Use a map of your town.
Make dialogues and act them out with a partner:

A: Excuse me, please. How can I get from
   the school to …?
B: Turn … and go along … Turn into …
   The … is on the …
A: Thank you.
B: You're welcome.

> the next bus stop •
> a hairdresser's •
> the park • …*straße* •
> a supermarket •
> …*weg* • …

7 Telling the way at your school

a ✏️ Draw a map of your school. Mark the main entrance.

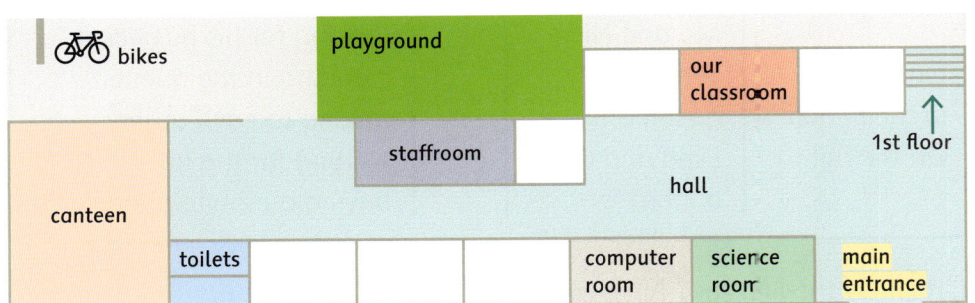

b 👥 ✏️ 💬 Make dialogues and act them out with a partner.

A: Excuse me. I'm looking for the staffroom.
   How can I get there?
B: Turn left and go along the hall.
   The staffroom is on the right.
A: Thank you.
B: You're welcome.

> our classroom •
> the canteen •
> the computer room •
> the science room •
> the toilets • …

Excuse me, please.
girl
boy
tourist

TIP: You can use
a free online map
of your town.

TIP: It can be helpful
to spell out proper
names like *Wilhelm-
straße*. For the letter
ß say 'double s'.
For *ä, ö, ü* say 'a (o, u)
with two dots'.

→ Module 2, p. 24
   (spelling words)

Thank you.
You're welcome.

→ My Words, pp. 66–67

TIP: Describe pictures like this:
1. Say where people and objects are:
   I can see a woman on the right.
   There's a man on the right.
   There are five people on the left.
2. Say what people are doing:
   Dina **is eating**.
   Yero and Mo **are playing** football.

1 Describing pictures

a ✎ What can you see the picture? Write in your exercise book.

I can see Mo, Nico, ... I can also see a bus stop, ...

b 👥💬 Compare with a partner.

c ✂ Match the sentences.

I can see a woman.
There's a man.
There are five people.

under ↔ on
in front of ↔ behind
in the middle
on the left
on the right
between ... and ...
shoe shop

1 I can see Olga.	**A** It's between the cafe and the shoe shop.
2 I can see Dina.	**B** She's in front of Dina.
3 I can see Yero's bus ticket.	**C** They're in front of the shoe shop.
4 There's a mobile phone shop.	**D** She's next to the bus stop.
5 There are Mo and Nico.	**E** She's behind Olga.
6 There's a woman.	**F** It's under his shoe.

d ✎ Write five sentences in your exercise book.

On the left In the middle On the right	Mo and Nico Yero a woman Dina and Olga a man	is are	looking for his bus ticket. standing in the queue. talking to each other. waiting for the bus. buying a mobile phone.

On the right Mo and Nico are ...

2 Describe your picture

a ✎ Draw a picture like.

b 👥💬✎ Don't show your picture to your partner, but describe it. Can your partner draw a sketch of your picture?

your picture

your partner's sketch

→ My Words, pp. 66–67

Checkpoint

1 ✏ Write the transport phrases.

| 1 | 2 | 3 | 4 | 5 | 6 |

1 _____   3 _____   5 _____

2 _____   4 _____   6 _____

2 🔊61 ✏ Look and listen. Is the information right or wrong? Tick.

1 The information is … ◯ right. ◯ wrong.

2 The information is … ◯ right. ◯ wrong.

3 The information is … ◯ right. ◯ wrong.

Dean Street · Market Street · Avon Street

3 ✏ Describe the way from the cafe to the park in 2.

Turn right and go along _____

_____

_____

4 ✏ Complete the sentences with the present progressive.

Yero and his little sister are in the park. Yero _____ (chat) with

his friends. And he _____ (look for) his bus ticket. Yero's sister

_____ (not look for) the bus ticket. She _____ (play).

Are his friends _____ (help) him? Yes, they _____ (be).

Dina and Olga _____ (help). But Mo and Nico _____

(not help). They _____ (go) to the cinema. Yero's bus ticket

_____ (lie) under his little sister's books!

5 ✏ Present progressive or simple present? Mark the right verb form.

Selma usually **is having / has** fun at home. She always **is playing / plays**
with her sisters. They often **are playing / play** hairdresser. They often
study / are studying English together. But not today! Selma's sister
is going / goes to the hospital today. Selma **is lying / lies** on the couch now.
She **is thinking / thinks** about her sister: Good luck, Sister!

5 Getting around town

English	German	My notes
What are you doing?	Was machst du (gerade)? / Was macht ihr (gerade)?	
I'm lying in the park.	Ich liege (gerade) im Park.	
I'm looking for my bus ticket.	Ich suche (gerade) meine Busfahrkarte.	
Are you having fun? Yes, I am./No, I'm not. Yes, we are./No, we aren't.	Hast du (gerade) Spaß?/ Habt ihr (gerade) Spaß? Ja./Nein.	
(right) now	jetzt (gerade)	
at the moment	im Moment, im Augenblick	
today	heute	
Getting around town:	**Sich in der Stadt bewegen:**	
(to) wait for the bus	auf den Bus warten	
(to) go to the park	in den Park gehen	
(to) sit at the bus stop	an der Bushaltestelle sitzen	
(to) lie in the park	im Park liegen	
(to) stand in the queue	anstehen, Schlange stehen	
(to) buy snacks	Snacks kaufen	
(to) help sb.	jm. helfen	
(to) come	kommen	
(to) drink water	Wasser trinken	
(to) eat a sandwich	ein belegtes Brot essen	

Places in town (Orte in der Stadt)
cafe das Café • **cinema** das Kino • **bike shop** der Fahrradladen •
bus stop die Bushaltestelle • **hairdresser's** der Friseurladen •
Jill's flat Jills Wohnung • **mobile phone shop** der Handyladen •
park der Park • **shoe shop** der Schuhladen • **shopping centre**
das Einkaufszentrum • **supermarket** der Supermarkt

boy	der Junge	
girl	das Mädchen	
tourist	der Tourist/die Touristin	

My Words

English	German	My notes
(to) talk to each other	miteinander sprechen	
(to) get ready for school	sich für die Schule fertig machen	

Means of transport (Verkehrsmittel)
(to) walk gehen • **(to) go by bike** Fahrrad fahren •
(to) go by car Auto fahren • **(to) go by bus** Bus fahren •
(to) go by train Zug fahren • **(to) go by scooter** Roller fahren

Asking and telling the way:	**Nach dem Weg fragen und den Weg beschreiben:**	
Excuse me, please.	Entschuldige bitte. / Entschuldigen Sie bitte.	
How can you get from … to …?	Wie kommt man von … zu/nach …?	
Thank you. You're welcome.	Danke. Gern geschehen.	
Go along the street.	Gehe die Straße entlang. / Gehen Sie …	
Turn right. / Turn left.	Biege rechts/links ab. / Biegen Sie rechts/links ab.	
on the road **in** the street	auf der Straße	

Describing pictures:	**Bilder beschreiben:**	
I can see a woman.	Ich sehe eine Frau.	
There's a man. **There are** five people.	Da ist ein Mann. Da sind fünf Personen.	
in the middle	in der Mitte	
on the left ↔ on the right	links ↔ rechts	
in front of ↔ behind	vor ↔ hinter	
on ↔ under	auf ↔ unter	
next to	neben	
near	in der Nähe von	
between … and …	zwischen … und …	

6 Planning a fashion show

What outfits are you going to present?

Our group is going to present beautiful dresses.

I'm going to make it shorter.

(to) plan a fashion show

(to) use sth.

(to) sew sth. on sth.

We're going to present the coolest T-shirts in the world.

We're going to wear disco outfits.

Are you going to buy all these clothes?

No, we aren't.

Clothes:
dress
trousers *(pl)*
T-shirt
shirt
sunglasses *(pl)*
shoe

Adjectives:
boring
beautiful ↔ ugly
cheap ↔ expensive
old ↔ new
big ↔ small
long ↔ short
colourful
cool
free
funny
second-hand

(to) send sth.

→ My Words, pp. 78–79

1 Planning a fashion show

🔊 62 📖 ✏️ Listen to and read the dialogues on page 68. Tick.

the dialogues on page 68

	right	wrong
1 The class is going to have a fashion show.	◯	◯
2 Olga and Maria are going to use new clothes.	◯	◯
3 Yero's group is going to have the most expensive outfits.	◯	◯
4 Jill's dad is going to send some second-hand clothes.	◯	◯

TIP:
1. Read the sentences.
2. Listen to or read the dialogues again.
3. Tick the right answers.
4. Check your answers.

2 What are they going to use?

a ✏️ 🔊 63 📖 Look at the pictures. Write *Y* for Yero, *O* for Olga and *M* for Mo. Listen and check your answers.

buttons

shoes

a shirt

a dress

paint

sunglasses

a T-shirt

trousers

Clothes and fashion:
button
paint
dress
trousers *(pl)*
shirt
T-shirt
shoe
sunglasses *(pl)*

is or *looks*
The T-shirt **is** new.
The T-shirt **looks** new.

b 🔊 64 📖 ✂️ Listen and read. Match the sentence parts.

1 The T-shirt is …   **A** very cool.
2 The trousers are …   **B** boring.
3 The sunglasses look …   **C** too long.
4 The shirt looks …   **D** new.

The T-shirt is new.

boring

very and too

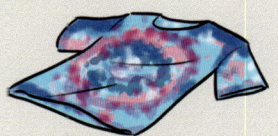

The T-shirt is **very** colourful.

The shirt is **too** big.

3 What do you think?

✏️ Write four or more sentences in your exercise book.

I think the	dress • paint • T-shirt	is looks	very too	big • boring • cool • cheap • colourful • beautiful • small • ugly • expensive • …
	buttons • shoes • sunglasses • trousers	are look		

I think the dress is too colourful and the trousers are ..

→ My Words, pp. 78–79

6   Planning a fashion show

1 The *going to*-future: positive and negative statements

📑 ✏ Read the boxes. Complete the sentences with the *going to*-future.

| I'm (= am)
You're (=are)
He/She/It's (= is)
We're
You're
They're | going to | help them.
buy it.
make it. | I'm not
You aren't
He/She/It isn't
We aren't
You aren't
They aren't | going to | help them.
buy it.
make it. |

| You form the *going to*-future with (not) am/are/is going to and the infinitive of the verb:
Yero's going to ask his mum for help.
We're not going to buy all these clothes. | You use going to to talk about intentions or plans for the future:
The groups are going to present their outfits at the fashion show in three weeks. |

1 Mo's group *is going to present* ____ (present) fashion of the 70s.

2 The students _____ (wear) cool outfits.

3 They _____ (not wear) hippie clothes.

4 They _____ (dress) like 70s disco dancers.

5 The group _____ (not buy) all clothes.

6 Jill's dad _____ (send) some second-hand clothes.

2 The *going to*-future: questions and short answers

📑 ✏ Read the boxes. Then match the questions to the answers.

| Am I
Are you
Is he/she/it
Are we
Are you
Are they | going to | help me?
buy it?
make it? | Yes, | I am.
we/you/they are.
he/she/it is. |
| | | | No, | I'm not.
we/you/they aren't.
he/she/it isn't. |

What are you going to present?

Questions with question words
What are you going to present?
How are you going to do this?
Who is going to help you?
→ Module 3, p.33 (question words)

1 What are you going to present?

2 Are you going to buy T-shirts?

3 Is Mr Chan going to help you?

4 Who is going to help you?

A No, we aren't.
   They're free.

B The coolest and
   cheapest T-shirts!

C My mum.

D No he isn't.

3 The comparison of adjectives: -er/-est, more/most

a 📖 Read the boxes.

Adjectives (like *good*, *beautiful*, *old*) say how people or things are or what they look like.	Adjectives can go before nouns or after verbs like *be* or *look*: This is a beautiful dress. This dress looks beautiful.

b 📖 ✏ Read the box. Complete the table with the right adjective forms.

Basic form: The blue button is as big as the green button.	**Comparative with -er:** The green button is bigger than the yellow button.	**Superlative with -est:** The red button is the biggest.

You use -er/-est with one-syllable adjectives: cool → cooler, coolest
You also use -er/-est with two-syllable adjectives ending in -y: fun·ny → funnier, funniest

basic form	comparative	superlative
cool	_____	_____
old	_____	_____
big	bigger	_____
ugly	uglier	_____

c 📖 ✏ Read the box and complete the table.

Some adjectives have two or more syllables: bo·ring, ex·pen·sive, beau·ti·ful	With these adjectives you use more and most: A T-shirt is more expensive than a button. This is the most expensive T-shirt in the shop.

basic form	comparative	superlative
expensive	more expensive	most expensive
beautiful	more beautiful	_____
boring	_____	_____

d 📖 🔊 65 💬 Read the box. Listen and repeat.

Some adjectives have irregular comparison forms, for example: good: better, best   bad: worse, worst   much, many: more, most

Clothes:
jacket
pullover
skirt
sock
jeans (*pl*)
boot
trainer

1 Talking about clothes

a 🔊66 📖 💬 Look at the pictures. Then listen, read and repeat.

b 🔊67 ✏ What do Olga and Yero say about the clothes?
Listen and number the adjectives (1–8).

| 1 a sweatshirt | 2 jeans | 3 boots | 4 a jacket |
| 5 a skirt | 6 trainers | 7 socks | 8 a pullover |

2 ☑ cool   ☐ boring   ☐ good   ☐ expensive

☐ beautiful ☐ colourful ☐ funny   ☐ ugly

c ✏ Mark the adjectives in 1b: comparative and superlative with
-er and -est, with *more* and *most* or irregular. Look at page 71 for help.

d ✏ Compare the clothes. Write six or more sentences in your
exercise book.

The	sweatshirt • skirt • jacket • pullover	looks	...-er than	the	boots • skirt • jacket • jeans • pullover • ...
	jeans • boots • socks • trainers	look	more ... than		

The trainers look better than the boots.

e 👥 💬 Talk to a partner.

I think the boots look better than the trainers.

I think the trainers look cooler than the boots.

2 Thinking about languages

👥 📖 💬 Look up these clothes words in a dictionary – German and your
languages. Are they similar or different? Talk in a group.

| pullover | T-shirt | blouse | jeans | top | sweatshirt |

TIP: There are free online dictionaries for most languages.
You can also use the online English-German dictionary for this workbook.

→ My Words, pp. 78–79

3 Clothes and money

a ◀》68 ✓ Look at the picture and listen. Tick the right answers.

◯ The clothes are all second hand.

◯ The shoes were more expensive than the jacket.

◯ Jill's dad is going to come to the fashion show.

◯ Jill is going to send her dad photos of the fashion show.

all (the) clothes

money
pound
penny *pl* pence

b ◀》69 ✓ How much were these clothes? Listen and write.

1 The shirt was _£2_____ .

2 The jeans were _____ .

3 The jacket was _____ .

4 The T-shirt was _____ .

5 The shoes were _____ .

6 The sunglasses were _____ .

British money

You write	You say
1p	one p [piː]
20p	twenty p
£1.50	one fifty
£5	five pounds
£10.90	ten ninety

How much is the shirt?
The shirt is £2.
How much are the shoes?
The shoes are £10.

c ▤ ✓ Check the sentences from 3b. What's <u>the most expensive</u> or <u>the cheapest</u> piece of clothing? Complete the sentences.

1 cheap: T-shirt, shoes or shirt?

The _T-shirt is the_____ piece of clothing.

2 expensive: shirt, shoes or jeans?

The _____ piece of clothing.

3 cheap: T-shirt, jeans or sunglasses?

The _____ piece of clothing.

Clothes
The word clothes has no singular form and you can't count it:

clothes *(pl)*

a piece of clothing *(sg)*

two pieces of clothing *(pl)*

4 Thinking about cultures

✓ ✋ Britain has pounds and pence. What about Germany and other countries? Make a poster about money in different countries.

(to) ask sb. for sth.

(to) phone sb.

(to) cut sth.

(to) work on a project

sewing tools *(pl)*

5 What are Olga's plans for this week?

🔊 70 📑 ✏️ Look, listen and read. Complete the sentences with the *going to*-future.

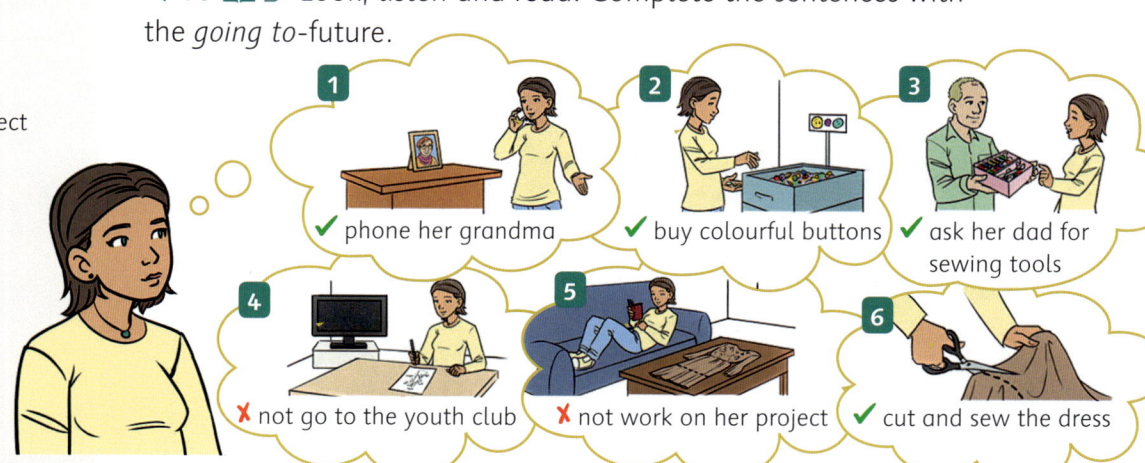

1 ✓ phone her grandma   2 ✓ buy colourful buttons   3 ✓ ask her dad for sewing tools

4 ✗ not go to the youth club   5 ✗ not work on her project   6 ✓ cut and sew the dress

English and German
Yero **is going to** ask his mum for help.
Yero **wird**/**will** seine Mutter um Hilfe **bitten**.

1 Olga _____ on Monday.

2 She _____ on Tuesday.

3 She _____ on Wednesday.

4 She _____ on Thursday.

5 She _____ on Friday.

6 She _____ on Saturday and Sunday.

6 Your plans for the weekend

a ✏️ Write three sentences about your plans for Saturday and Sunday.

> do my homework • go to the gym • go swimming • go to the youth club • meet my friends • visit my grandma/aunt/… • watch TV • …

I'm going to _____

_____

_____

TIP: Change the green words in the dialogue:
I'm going to go to the youth club on Saturday.
→ *I'm going to meet my friends on Saturday.*

What about you?
Me too.

→ My Words, pp. 78–79

b 👥 💬 Talk to two or more partners. Do they have the same plans?

I'm going to go to the youth club on Saturday. What about you?

Me too.

I'm going to go swimming.

7 Plan your own fashion project and present it

a ◀)) 71 ▤ ／ Listen, read and look. Number the texts (1–4).

Finally, I'm going to sew the shirt and the T-shirt together. My friend Leila ist going to help me. ◯

Today I'm going to present my fashion project 'T-blouse'. I'm going to use an old T-shirt, one of my dad's old shirts and some sewing tools. ◯

First I'm going to cut off the upper part and the cuffs of the shirt. Then I'm going to cut off the lower part of the T-shirt. ◯

In this picture you can see my new 'T-blouse'. I like it because looks beautiful. And it's unique – nobody has a blouse like this! ◯

Giving a short talk:
Today I'm going to talk about …

First …

Then …

Finally, …

That s the end of my presentation.

Thank you for listening.

Do you have any questions?

TIP: Look up more words in an online dictionary.

b ／ Make notes for your presentation.

1 Today I'm going to present my fashion project '…'

2 I'm going to use …
old shoes • paint • my dad's old hat • second-hand clothes • sewing tools • …

1. What fashion project are you going to present?
2. What are you going to use?
3. How are you going to make it?
4. What is special about your new outfit? Why do you like it?
5. End your presentation.

3 First I'm going to …
Then I'm going to …
Finally, I'm going to …
get • cut (off) • draw • buy • sew • …

4 In this picture you can see my new '…'
I like it because it's beautiful • very cheap • cool • …

5 That's the end of my presentation.
Thank you for listening.
Do you have any questions?

c 👥 💬 Present your project in a group.

→ My Words, pp. 78–79

1 How to plan and give a short talk

a ✏ Prepare a short talk about fashion: your favourite outfit, a celebrity's outfit or a traditional costume. Collect your ideas in this mind map:

traditional costume

TIP: Look at pages 69, 72 and 75 for more words and phrases. Look up more words in an online dictionary.

→ M2, p. 26 (Online dictionaries and apps)

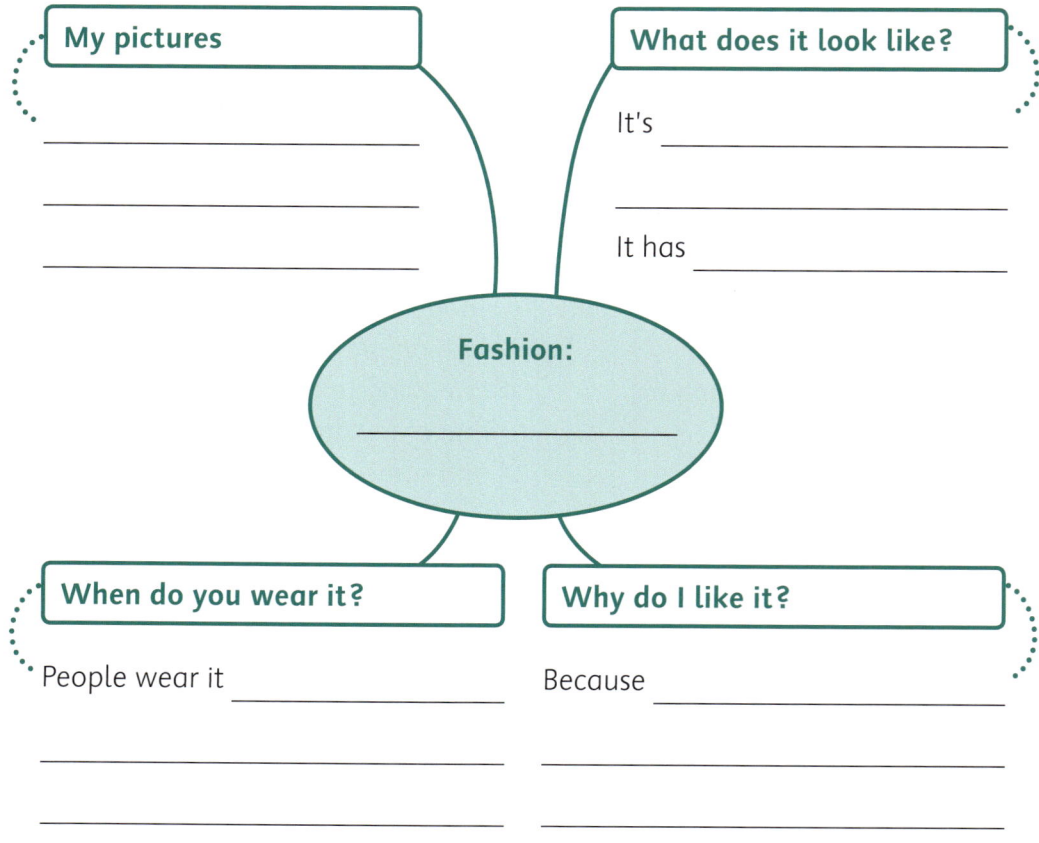

My pictures

_____
_____
_____

What does it look like?

It's _____
_____

It has _____

Fashion:

_____

When do you wear it?

People wear it _____
_____
_____

Why do I like it?

Because _____
_____
_____

TIP: How to plan and give a short talk:
1. Collect ideas in a mind map, in a list or on cards.
2. Plan your talk and write down typical phrases.
3. Practise your talk alone or with a partner.
4. Give your talk in a group or in class.

Today I'm going to talk about …
Now I'm going to tell you …
That's the end of my talk.

TIP: Listen again to Olga's talk. You can use her phrases. Change her ideas for your own ideas.

b 📖 ✏ Read the phrases for a short talk. Number the phrases (1–7).

⭘ Do you have any questions?   ⭘ Finally, I'm going tell you …

⭘ First I'm going to show you some pictures.

⭘ Thank you for listening.   ① Today I'm going to talk about …

⭘ Now I'm going to tell you …   ⭘ That's the end of my talk.

c 🔊72 ✏ Listen to Olga's short talk and check your answers. Copy the phrases 1–6 in your exercise book.

d 🔊72 ✏ Listen again. Make notes on cards. Use your ideas from 1a and the phrases from 1b.

Today I'm going to talk about my grandma's sarafan.

First I'm going to show you some pictures: A woman with a sarafan and some matryoshka dolls.

Now I'm going to tell you what the sarafan looks like. It's a long apron dress. It has …

e 👥💬 Practise your talk alone or with a partner.

→ My Words, pp. 78–79
f 👥💬 Give your talk in a group.

1 🔊73 ✏️ Listen and tick the clothes that Jill is going to buy.

2 ✏️ Complete the sentences with the *going to*-future.

1 Jill _____ a rugby match.

2 She _____ to the cinema.

3 She _____ a new dress.

4 She _____ her dad.

> Plans for the weekend:
> – watch rugby match ✔
> – go to cinema ✘
> – buy new dress ✘
> – phone Dad ✔

3 ✏️ Complete the sentences with the right forms of the adjectives.

short

The red skirt is _____ than the pink skirt.

The blue skirt is the _____ .

expensive

£32 £20 £45

The brown jacket is _____ than the blue jacket.

The black jacket is the _____ .

big

The pink socks are _____ than the yellow socks.

The green socks are the _____ .

4 ✏️ What's the right order? Number the phrases.

◯ Do you have any questions?

◯ First I'm going to show you some pictures.

◯ Finally, I'm going tell you why I like my outfit.

◯ That's the end of my talk.

◯ Today I'm going to talk about my favourite outfit.

◯ Thank you for listening.

◯ Now I'm going to tell you what my outfit looks like.

English	German	My notes
What outfits are you going to present?	Welche Outfits werdet/wollt ihr präsentieren?	
Our group is going to present beautiful dresses.	Unsere Gruppe wird/will schöne Kleider präsentieren.	
I'm going to make the dress shorter.	Ich werde/will das Kleid kürzer machen.	
We're going to present the coolest T-shirts in the world.	Wir werden/wollen die coolsten T-Shirts der Welt präsentieren.	
We're going to wear disco outfits.	Wir werden/wollen Disco-Kleidung tragen.	
Are you going to buy all these clothes? No, we aren't./Yes, we are.	Werdet/Wollt ihr all diese Kleider kaufen? Nein./Ja.	
(to) plan a fashion show	eine Modenschau planen	
(to) use sth. (for sth.)	etw. (für etw.) benutzen	
(to) sew sth. on sth.	etw. an etw. nähen	

Clothes and fashion (Kleidung und Mode)
boot der Stiefel • **button** der Knopf • **costume** das Kostüm, die Verkleidung • **dress** das Kleid • **paint** die (Textil-)Farbe • **pullover** der Pullover • **sewing tools** *(pl)* das Nähzeug • **shirt** das Hemd • **skirt** der Rock • **shoe** der Schuh • **sock** die Socke • **sunglasses** *(pl)* die Sonnenbrille • **jacket** die Jacke • **trainer** der Turnschuh • **trousers** *(pl)* die Hose • **T-shirt** das T-Shirt

The T-shirt is **very** colourful.	Das T-Shirt ist sehr bunt.	
The shirt is **too** big.	Das Hemd ist zu groß.	
The T-shirt **is** new. The T-shirt **looks** new.	Das T-Shirt ist neu. Das T-Shirt sieht neu aus.	

Adjectives (Adjektive)
beautiful (wunder)schön • **big** groß • **boring** langweilig • **cheap** billig • **colourful** bunt, farbig • **cool** cool • **expensive** teuer • **free** kostenlos; frei • **funny** lustig • **long** lang • **new** neu • **old** alt • **second-hand** aus zweiter Hand, gebraucht • **small** klein • **short** kurz • **traditional** traditionell • **ugly** hässlich

English	German	My notes
good, better, the best	gut, besser, der/die/das beste	
bad, worse, the worst	schlecht, schlecher, der/die/das schlechteste	
much/many, more, the most	viel, mehr, der/die/das meiste	
clothes (pl)	die Kleidung, die Kleidungsstücke (Pl.)	
clothing a piece of clothing	die Kleidung das Kleidungsstück	
money	das Geld	
pound (£) penny, pl pence (pennies)	das Pfund (britische Währung) der Penny	
How much is the shirt? The shirt is £2. How much are the shoes? The shoes are £10.	Wieviel kostet das Hemd? Das Hemd kostet 2 Pfund. Wieviel kosten die Schuhe? Die Schuhe kosten 10 Pfund.	
What about you?	Und du? / Und Sie?	
Me too.	Ich auch.	
(to) ask sb. for sth. (to) ask sb. for help	jn. um etwas bitten jn. um Hilfe bitten	
(to) phone sb.	jn. anrufen	
(to) cut sth.	etwas schneiden, abschneiden	
(to) work on a project	an einem Projekt arbeiten	
Giving a short talk:	**Einen Kurzvortrag halten:**	
Today I'm going to present/ talk about …	Heute präsentiere/ spreche ich über …	
First I'm going to show you some pictures.	Zuerst werde ich euch ein paar Bilder zeigen.	
Finally,/Now I'm going to tell you …	Zuletzt/Jetzt werde ich euch sagen …	
That's the end of my talk/ presentation.	Das war mein Vortrag/ meine Präsentation.	
Thank you for listening.	Danke für's Zuhören.	
Do you have any questions?	Habt ihr noch Fragen?	

international food buffet

We've made the fruit salad.

Have you cut the bread yet?

No, I haven't./Yes, I have.

But I've just cut the vegetables.

What have you done so far?

(to) bake
(to) clean
(to) cook
(to) try

(to) do,
past participle: done

(to) drink,
past participle: drunk

(to) eat,
past participle: eaten

(to) make,
past participle: made

(to) put,
past participle: put

(to) see,
past participle: seen

I've never seen so much food.

Have you ever eaten tabouleh before?

Food:
bread
fruit
cake
salad
soup
olive

Drink:
tea
juice
water
milk

cold
delicious
yummy *(infml)*

→ My Words, pp. 92–93

1 Is everything ready for the international food buffet?

a 🔊 74 📖 Look at page 80. Listen and read.

b 📖 ✂️ Who has done what? Read again. Match the sentence parts.

c ✏️ Number the pictures (1–5).

1 Yero and Maria	**A** has just cut the vegetables. **(1)**
2 Mo	**B** has already cleaned the table. **(2)**
3 Olga	**C** has eaten all the tabculeh. **(3)**
4 Pablo	**D** have already made the fruit salad. **(4)**
	E hasn't cut the bread yet. **(5)**

   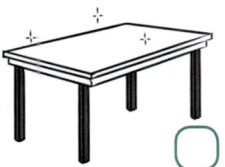 

2 Fruit and vegetables

a 📖 ✏️ Read and write the words from the box in the food network.

~~apple~~ • banana • bell pepper • ~~carrot~~ • cucumber • lemon • orange • strawberry • tomato

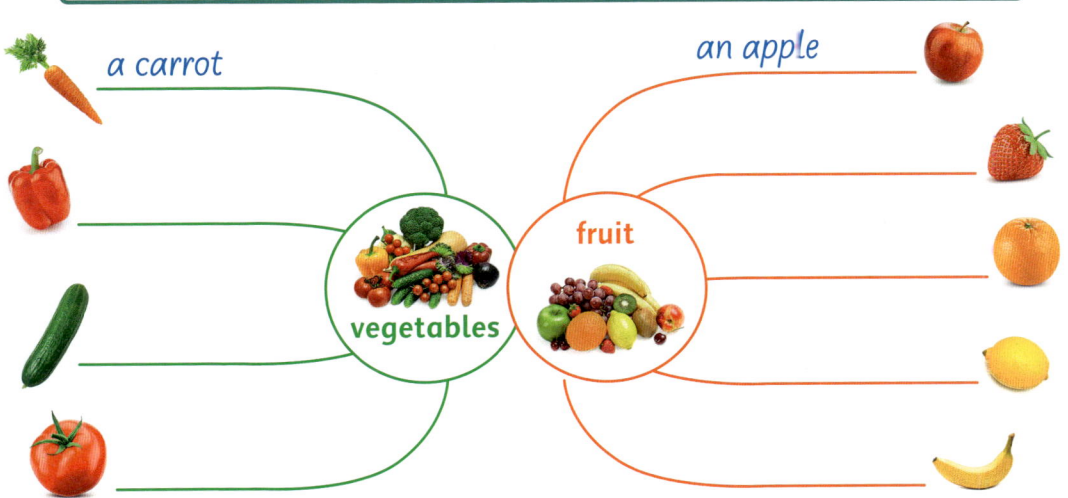

a carrot

an apple

fruit

vegetables

b 🔊 75 📖 Listen and check.

c ✏️ What have you eaten this week? Complete the sentence with two vegetables or fruits.

I've eaten some _____

d 👥 💬 Compare with a partner. Has he or she eaten the same food?

I've eaten some strawberries and tomatoes this week. What about you?

I haven't eaten any strawberries this week. But I've eaten some tomatoes and bananas.

Fruit and vegetables:

🍏 apple

🍌 banana

🫑 bell pepper

🥕 carrot

🥒 cucumber

🍋 lemon

🍊 orange

🍓 strawberry, pl strawberries

🍅 tomato, pl tomatoes

a or an?
Check how you **say** the next word:
a carrot
an apple

With **A, E, I, O, U** you say **an**.

→ Sounds, p. 110

I've eaten some …
I haven't eaten any …

→ My Words, pp. 92–93

7   International food buffet

1 The present perfect: positive statements

a ▣ ✏ ꕥ Read the boxes. Then complete the sentences with regular present perfect forms.
Match sentences 1–3 to sentences A–C.

I've (= have) You've He/She/It's (= has) We've You've They've	baked. cleaned. cooked.

You form the present perfect of regular verbs with have/has and the past participle with -ed.
⚠ Be careful with the spelling of these verbs:
bake: baked
stop: stopped
try: tried (but: play – played)

I've cleaned the table. Now we can put the drinks on it.
Jill has cooked tomato soup. It looks yummy!

You use the present perfect to say that something has or hasn't happened at some time in the past. There's often an effect on the present.

1 The students _____ (clean) all the tables.

2 Mr Chan _____ (try) the Jollof rice.

3 Yero _____ (finish) all his tasks.

A But it's too spicy for him.

B Now he's tired, but happy.

C Now people can eat there.

b ▣ ✏ Read the box. Complete the table with irregular past participle forms from page 80.

I've (= have) You've He/She/It's (= has) We've You've They've	eaten vegetables. drunk water. been very nice.

You form the present perfect of irregular verbs with have/has and the past participle of the verb. There is no rule for the past participle of irregular verbs. You need to learn them.

→ Irregular verbs, pp. 108–109

infinitive	simple past	past participle
be	was / were	been
have	had	had
do	did	_____
cut	cut	_____
drink	drank	_____
eat	ate	_____
make	made	_____
see	saw	_____

c ✏ Complete the sentences with irregular present perfect forms.

1 I _____ (eat) too much cake!

2 We _____ (do) the shopping.

3 Mo _____ (cut) the bread now.

4 Sina _____ (make) a tomato salad.

5 She ___ never _____ (be) to the canteen.

6 They _____ (have) lots of fun so far.

2 The present perfect: negative statements

a ▦ ✏ ♆ Read the boxes. Then complete the sentences with *haven't* or *hasn't*.
Match sentences 1–4 to sentences A–D.

I haven't You haven't He/She/It hasn't We haven't You haven't They haven't	baked. cleaned. cooked. eaten. drunk.

You make negative statements in the present perfect with haven't/hasn't and the past participle of the verb.

With negative statements in the present perfect, you often use yet or before.

1 The students _____ finished their project.

2 I _____ seen the film yet.

3 Yero _____ studied for the test yet.

4 You _____ done your homework yet.

5 Olga _____ eaten lasagne before.

A But she really likes it.

B So you can't go to the cinema.

C Have you seen it?

D They're still working on it.

E He's going to study at the weekend.

b ✏ Complete the sentences with the positive and negative forms of the present perfect.
Be careful with the irregular verbs.

1 Jill *has been* to the supermarket.

But she _____ to the copy shop yet.

2 She _____ the chocolate cake.

But she _____ the lemon cake yet.

3 Pablo _____ carrot juice before.

But he _____ cucumber juice.

4 They _____ the tables.

But they _____ the chairs yet.

1 ✔ be | not be ✗   2 ✔ make | not make ✗

3 ✔ try | not try ✗   4 ✔ clean | not clean ✗

c ✏ What have or haven't you done this week? Write sentences.

1 (not) eat | enough fruit | enough vegetables

I've eaten

_____

2 (not) do | all my homework | exercises

_____

_____

3 (not) use | a smartphone | a computer

_____

_____

3 The present perfect: questions and short answers

a 📖 ✏ 🎯 Read the boxes. Then write the questions. Match the questions to the answers.

Have	I you we you they	eaten yet? helped you? been here?
Has	he/she/it	

Yes,	I you	have.
No,	we/you/they	haven't.
Yes,	he/she/it	has.
No,		hasn't.

Questions with question words
What have you done?
Where has he been?
Who has cut the bread?

Where have you been?

I've been here in the canteen.

1 been | ~~Where~~ | you | have | ?

   Where _____

   A Because Jill wanted to cut it.

2 the cake | haven't | cut | you | Why | yet | ?

   _____

   B No, I haven't. Jill is going to show them to me.

3 you | tried | the food | Have | ?

   _____

   C I've been here in the canteen.

4 seen | you | Jill's photos | Have | ?

   _____

   D Yes, I have. I've tried all the salads.

b 🔊 76 📖 Listen to the dialogue and check your answers.

4 Signal words: adverbs of indefinite time

📖 ✏ Read the box. Then mark the right answers.

I've **already** eaten. We've **just** come home. I've **never** eaten tabouleh **before**. I've seen the film **before**. Mo **hasn't cut** the bread **yet**. Have you **ever** drunk tomato juice? Have you cut the bread **yet**?	The present perfect tells you that something has or hasn't happened. You don't know when it happened. With the present perfect you can only use adverbs of indefinite time like: already never ever? just not ... yet yet? before often

1 Which two adverbs stand at the <u>end</u> of a sentence?

already • before • ever • just • never • often • yet

2 Which four adverbs <u>aren't</u> signal words for the present perfect?

already • an hour ago • ever • just • last week • never • on Monday • yesterday

5 Present perfect or simple past?

a 📖 ✏ Read the blue boxes.
Complete the sentences with
the verb forms from the green box.

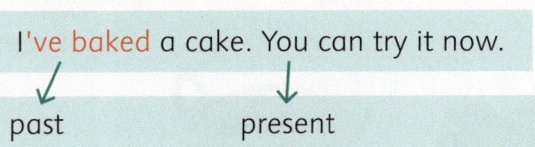

> I've baked a cake for the buffet.
> You can try it now.
> I baked it yesterday
> I used lots of chocolate.

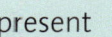

I've baked a cake. You can try it now.

↓   ↓

past   present

I baked it yesterday.
I used lots of chocolate.

↓

past   present

You use the present perfect to say that something has happened in the past. It isn't important when it happened. You're thinking about the past and the present. You often use signal words like already, just, ever, never, yet, …

You use the simple past to say when something happened in the past. You're only thinking about the past. You often use signal words like yesterday, in 2018, last week, ten minutes ago, …

→ Module 4, p.44

> did … make | 've made • tried | haven't tried • finished | Have … finished •
> Did … clean | 've … cleaned

1 **I've made** a chocolate cake for the buffet. – When _____ you _____ it?

2 I _____ the lemon cake yet, but I _____ the chocolate cake this morning.

3 _____ you _____ your homework yet? – Yes, I _____ it ten minutes ago.

4 _____ you _____ the table this morning? – No, but I _____ just _____ it.

b 📖 ✏ Read Mo's text and mark the right verb forms.

My first day at school in Germany

My first day at school in Germany **have been / was** after I moved here last summer. In Syria I **haven't gone / didn't go** to school for a year. Last summer I **have come / came** to Germany with my brother.
I like this school because most of the teachers and students are nice. I**'ve made / made** lots of new friends. Olga and Yero are my best friends in class. I**'ve learned / learned** a lot too. Mr Chan says that my German **has improved / improved** a lot. And Jill says that my English **has improved / improved** too. I usually don't study at the weekend. But last weekend I**'ve studied / studied** English with Olga and Yero. It **has been / was** fun!

c ✏ Write four or more sentences about yourself. You can use the text from 4b.
My first day at school in Germany was in August 2018 …

d 👥 💬 Compare your sentences with a partner.

(to) cook

Food and meals:
cereal
biscuit
vegetable curry
fish and chips *(pl)*
meat
pasta with tomato sauce
yoghurt
cheese
potato, *pl* potatoes

English and German	
E	G
biscuit	Keks
cake	Kuchen

Describing food:
sweet
spicy
salty
hot
cold
I'm allergic to …

1 Dad's cooking

a 🔊 77 📑 ✏️ Jill's dad is in Germany for two weeks. He cooks for Jill every day. What has Jill eaten so far? Listen, read and tick.

⬜ pasta with tomato sauce
⬜ yoghurt
⬜ cheese
⬜ vegetable curry
⬜ fish and chips
⬜ meat
⬜ potatoes
⬜ biscuits
⬜ cereal

b 🔊 77 ✏️ What's Jill's favourite food and what is she allergic to? Listen again and write.

Jill's favourite food is _____

Jill is allergic to _____

c 📑 ✂️ Look and read. Match the adjectives to the food.

| salty | sweet | cold | spicy | hot |

d 🔊 78 📑 Listen and check.

2 Your food

a ✏️ Copy and complete the mind map in your exercise book.

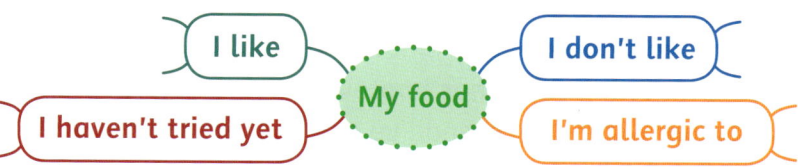

I like
I don't like
I haven't tried yet
My food
I'm allergic to

b ✏️ Write five or more sentences in your exercise book.
I like sweet food: biscuits, cake and chocolate. I also like spicy food: …

TIP: Look up more words in an online dictionary.

→ Module 2, p. 26 (Online dictionaries and apps)

→ My Words, pp. 92–93

c 👥 💬 Compare your sentences with a partner.

3 A checklist for the buffet

a Write the present perfect forms of the verbs with *he*.

TIP: You can look up the irregular past participle forms on pages 108–109.

ask – *he has asked*   clean – _____   write – _____

buy – _____   make – _____

b 📖 / Read Yero, Mo and Olga's checklists. What jobs have or haven't they done? Write in your exercise book.

Yero's jobs
– buy drinks ✔
– buy fruit ✘
– make puff-puffs ✘

Mo's jobs
– buy vegetables ✘
– make tabouleh ✘
– clean the room ✔

Olga's jobs
– write food signs ✔
– buy biscuits ✘
– clean the tables ✔

Yero has bought drinks and ... He hasn't ...

4 Your checklist for this week

a / Choose four jobs from the box. Write them in a table in your exercise book.

buy new pens for school • clean my bike • do all my homework • practise my instrument • study for the test • write a message to my best friend

	Me	Partner
study for the test	✔	
do all my homework		
...		

b / Tick the jobs that you have done already.
c / Write down the present perfect forms of the verbs in your checklist.

clean – *I've cleaned* _____   do – _____

study – _____   practise – _____

d 👥 💬 Find a partner and talk about your jobs.

I've studied for the test. What about you?

I haven't studied for the test. But I've done all my homework. What about you?

→ My Words, pp. 92–93

5 Street food is international

a 🔊 79 📑 ✏ Listen and read. Number the pictures (1–3).

1 Falafel are vegetable balls that come from Lebanon.
2 Ayran is a yoghurt drink that you drink cold.
3 Warga is a green tea that you drink sweet and very hot.

b ✏ Write about three or more foods in your exercise book.

burritos • burgers • crepes • currywurst • kumpir • tacos • …	is are	a food • a drink • a pasta • …	that	is very spicy/sweet/… comes from … you eat/drink hot/… is filled with …

Tacos are a traditional Mexican food that's filled with meat or vegetables.

c 👥 💬 Find a partner who knows about other food.

6 A game

a ✏ Write five or more cards.
b 👥 Play a game in class:
– Play in teams.
– The quizmaster reads the cards out loud.
– The teams answer: "It's …/They're …"
– The fastest team gets a point.

> It's a drink that you can drink hot or cold. It's white.
> (It's milk.)

> They're vegetable balls that come from Lebanon.
> (They're falafel.)

7 Thinking about cultures

a ✏ ✋ Make a poster about your favourite food or drink.
– What's your favourite food/drink?
– What is it? (pasta, meat, …)
– Is it spicy, sweet, …?
– Do you eat/drink it hot or cold?
– What country is it from?
b 👥 💬 Walk around in class and look at the posters. Talk to different partners about their favourite food and drink.

MY FAVOURITE FOOD

My favourite food is pelmeni. It's pasta that's filled with meat. It's not very spicy. You eat it hot. It's from Russia.

… is/are a drink/a food/ … that is …
– spicy/sweet/…
– comes from …
– you eat cold/drink hot/…
– filled with …

TIP: Do some research on the internet to find out more about your favourite food.

→ My Words, pp. 92–93

8 Interview: Have you ever eaten goat cheese?

a ✎ Complete questions 1 and 2 with two more food words.
b ✎ Write three more questions. You can use questions from 8d.
c ✎ Answer the questions for your yourself (*Me*).

Questions	Me	Partner
1 Have you ever eaten …		
– *goat cheese?*		
–		
–		
2 Have you ever drunk …		
– *ayran?*		
–		
–		
3		
4		
5		

d 👥 💬 ✎ Ask and answer your questions with a partner.
Write down his or her answers in the table in 8c.

> **TIP:** Change the green words and make your own sentences.

What's your favourite food?

Is it spicy/sweet/…?

What have you eaten today?

What did you eat yesterday?

What food are you allergic to?

My favourite food is pasta with tomato sauce.

It can be salty or spicy.

I've eaten cereal with milk and a sandwich.

I ate a sandwich, falafel, a salad and a yoghurt.

I'm not allergic to any kind of food.

e 👥 ✋ 💬 Record or film your interview and present it to the class.

→ My Words, pp. 92–93

(to) forget,
past participle: forgotten

TIP: How to understand listening texts:
1. Look at the pictures and read the heading.
2. Read the tasks and other information.
3. Listen and do the tasks (use a pencil).
4. Listen again and check. Correct your mistakes.
5. You don't need to understand every word.

1 How to understand listening texts

a ✎ Look at the picture. What do you think the dialogue will be about? Tick.

○ Jill has forgotten to go shopping.

○ Jill has forgotten to buy something.

○ Jill can't read the shopping list.

b ◀)80 ▤ Listen and check your answer in 1a. Were you right?

c ▤ ◀)80 ✎ Read the sentences. Listen again and tick.

1 Jill is talking to …	○ her father.	○ her aunt.	○ her mother.
2 Jill is in …	○ Britain.	○ Germany.	○ Spain.
3 Jill didn't buy …	○ potatoes.	○ meat.	○ milk.

2 More listening: At the fruit bar

a ▤ Look at the poster. What fruit do you like?

b ◀)81 ✎ Who chooses what? Listen. Listen again and tick (✔) or cross (✘).

TIP: You can listen to the text one, two or more times.

	Olga	Mo	Yero
apples	✘		
bananas	✔		
lemons	✘		
oranges	✔		
strawberries	✔		

FRUIT BAR
Obstsalat, wie du ihn willst!
Stell dir euch aus drei Obstsorten deinen eigenen Obstsalat zusammen.
JETZT NEU!

c ◀)81 ✎ Why <u>don't</u> they eat some of the fruit? Listen again and make notes in your exercise book like this:
Olga: ✘ apples – allergic, ✘ lemons – doesn't like

d ✎ Write full answers in your exercise book. Use these phrases:

… doesn't eat	apples • bananas • lemons • oranges • strawberries	because	he/she's allergic to them. he/she doesn't like them.

Olga doesn't eat apples because she's allergic to them.
She doesn't eat lemons because she doesn't like them.

→ My Words, pp. 92–93

Checkpoint

1 ✏ Write down the food words.

1 _____   [1]   [2]   [3]
2 _____
3 _____
4 _____   [4]   [5]
5 _____

☺ ☐
😐 ☐
☹ ☐

2 📖 ✏ What's the right word? Read and write.

1 It's a green vegetable that you eat cold. You can make salad with it.

It's _____

2 It's a drink that you drink hot or cold. In England, people drink it a lot.

It's _____

☺ ☐
😐 ☐
☹ ☐

3 🔊 82 ✓ ✏ What has Mo done and what hasn't he done yet?

Listen and tick (✔) or cross (✗). Then write full sentences.

1 Mo _____
2 He _____
3 _____
4 _____

⬭ buy the fruit
⬭ cut the fruit
⬭ make tabouleh
⬭ clean the table

☺ ☐
😐 ☐
☹ ☐

4 ✏ Write the questions in the present perfect.

| you | (eat) | yet | the cake • what | (do) | you • (try) | ever | you | tomato salad |

1 _____ Yes, I have. It was really good!
2 _____ I've cleaned the tables.
3 _____ No, I haven't. I don't like tomatoes.

☺ ☐
😐 ☐
☹ ☐

5 📖 ✏ Read and mark the right verb form.

When Olga lived in Russia, she **has gone / went** to three different schools:
When she was eight, her family **has moved / moved** to a small town. When
she was ten, her family **has moved / moved** again. Last winter Olga **has
come / came** to Germany with her dad. She **hasn't spoken / didn't speak**
any German then. But she **has studied / studied** a lot and so her German
has improved / improved. Her English **has improved / improved** too!

☺ ☐
😐 ☐
☹ ☐

7 International food buffet

English	German	My notes
international food buffet	ein Büfett mit internationalen Gerichten	
We've made the fruit salad.	Wir haben den Obstsalat gemacht.	
Have you cut the bread yet?	Hast du schon das Brot geschnitten?	
No, I haven't. / Yes, I have.	Ja. / Nein.	
But I've just cut the vegetables.	Aber ich habe gerade das Gemüse geschnitten.	
I've already put tea on the table.	Ich habe schon Tee auf den Tisch gestellt.	
I've never seen so much food.	Ich habe noch nie so viel Essen gesehen.	
Have you ever eaten tabouleh before?	Hast du schon mal Tabouleh gegessen?	

Irregular past participles

be	was/were	been	sein; war; (ist) gewesen
cut	cut	cut	schneiden; schnitt; (hat) geschnitten
do	did	done	tun; tat; (hat) getan
drink	drank	drunk	trinken; trank; (hat) getrunken
eat	ate	eaten	essen; aß; (hat) gegessen
forget	forgot	forgotten	vergessen; vergaß; (hat) vergessen
go	went	gone	gehen; ging; (ist) gegangen
have	had	had	haben; hatte; (hat) gehabt
make	made	made	machen; machte; (hat) gemacht
put	put	put	legen; legte; (hat) gelegt
see	saw	seen	sehen; sah; (hat) gesehen

→ Irregular verbs, pp. 108–109

English	German	My notes
I've eaten **some** fruit.	Ich habe Obst gegessen.	
I **haven't** eaten **any** fruit.	Ich habe kein Obst gegessen.	
(to) bake	backen	
(to) clean	sauber machen, putzen	
(to) cook	kochen, (Essen) zubereiten	
(to) try	probieren, versuchen	

My Words

English	German	My notes
already • not … yet • yet? • never • ever? • just • before • so far		
Olga and Mo have **already** gone.	schon	
Olga has**n't** made the signs **yet**.	noch nicht	
Have you cut the vegetables **yet**?	schon	
I've **never** been to Britain.	noch nie	
Have you **ever** eaten fish?	schon mal	
I've **just** tried to phone her.	gerade (eben)	
I haven't eaten tabouleh **before**.	vorher	
I haven't seen Yero **so far**.	bis jetzt	
… is a drink/food/… that comes from/is filled with/…	… ist ein Getränk/Essen/…, das aus … kommt/mit … gefüllt ist/…	
I'm allergic to …	Ich bin allergisch gegen …	

Food (Essen)

vegetables	das Gemüse	fruit	das Obst
bell pepper	die Paprika	apple	der Apfel
carrot	die Karotte, die Möhre	banana	die Banane
		lemon	die Zitrone
cucumber	die Gurke	orange	die Orange
olive	die Olive	strawberry, pl strawberries	die Erdbeere
potato, pl potatoes	die Kartoffel		
tomato, pl tomatoes	die Tomate		

Meals (Mahlzeiten, fertige Gerichte)

fish and chips	Fisch mit Pommes	biscuit	der Keks
		bread	das Brot
meat	das Fleisch	cake	der Kuchen
pasta with tomato sauce	Nudeln mit Tomatensauce	cereal	die Frühstücks-flocken (Pl.)
salad	der Salat (zubereitet)	cheese	der Käse
		yoghurt	der Joghurt
soup	die Suppe		
vegetable curry	das Gemüse-curry		

Drinks (Getränke)

juice	der Saft	water	das Wasser
tea	der Tee	milk	die Milch

Describing food (Essen beschreiben)
sweet süß • **spicy** würzig, scharf • **salty** salzig • **hot** 1. heiß 2. sehr scharf • **cold** kalt • **delicious** köstlich • **yummy** lecker

8 Let's celebrate!

Let's celebrate.

I hope the weather will be good.

Maybe the other students won't like it (the dance show).

I'm worried about …

Don't worry.

Celebrations and parties:
decoration
food
buffet
show
party, *pl* parties

I hope it won't rain tomorrow.

Will there be enough parents to help?

I'll send it (the email) right now.

It'll be sunny and warm.

If it rains, the decorations will be ruined.

How will Mr Chan like my Jollof rice?

If your Jollof rice is too spicy for Mr Chan, he can eat your puff-puffs.

→ My Words, pp. 106–107

1 Don't worry – let's celebrate!

🔊 83 📖 ✏️ Listen to and read the dialogues on page 94.
Who is worried about what? Write in your exercise book.

┌─────────────────────────────┐
… is/are worried about … │ the dance show • the food • the weather │
└─────────────────────────────┘

2 Perfect weather for a party?

a 📖 🔊 84 ✏️ Read the weather words in the box. What's good party
weather for Jill? Listen and draw smileys: ☺ perfect   ☺ OK   ☹ bad

⚪ sunny and hot

⚪ rainy and cold

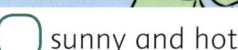

⚪ sunny and windy

⚪ sunny and warm

Weather words

☀️ sunny   🌧️ rainy

🎏 windy   ☁️ cloudy

🌡️ cold   🌡️ cool

🌡️ warm   🌡️ hot

Talking about the
weather:
sunny
windy
rainy
cloudy
cold
cool
warm
hot

perfect
OK
bad

b 👥 💬 What do you think? Talk to a partner.

It's perfect for a party
when it's hot and sunny.
What do you think?

I don't like it when it's hot.
I think it's perfect when it's
warm.

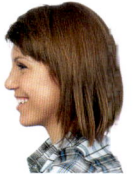

It's perfect for a party
when it's hot and sunny.

TIP: Change the green
words in the dialogue.

3 A happy ending for the party?

✏️ Complete the sentences with the words in the box.

┌──────────────────────────────────────┐
│ dance show • email • parents • party • weather │
└──────────────────────────────────────┘

outside ↔ inside

1 If Mo's group practises enough, the _____ will be great.

2 If Jill sends the _____ now, there will be enough _____
   at the party.

3 If the _____ is good, the _____ will be outside.

→ My Words, pp. 106–107

1 The *will*-future: positive and negative statements

a 📖 ✏️ Read the boxes. Then complete the sentences about the *will*-future.

I'll You'll He/She/It'll (= will) We'll You'll They'll	be worried. celebrate. come.	I You He/She/It We You They	won't (= will not)	be worried. celebrate. come.

You form the will-future with will/won't and the infinitive of the verb: It'll be sunny and warm tomorrow. I hope it won't rain. Maybe there won't be enough parents.	You use the will-future to say what you think or know about the future. There are often signal words like tomorrow, next week, … ⚠ Don't use the will-future to talk about plans for the future. For plans use the going to-future. → Module 6, p.70 (going to-future)

1 Use __will_____ or _____ and the infinitive in positive sentences.

2 Use _____ and the infinitive in negative sentences.

3 Use the _____ to say what you <u>think</u> about the future.

4 Use the _____ to say what you <u>plan</u> for the future.

> going to-future • 'll •
> ~~will~~ • will-future •
> won't

b 📖 ✏️ 🗣 Read page 94 again and complete the sentences.
Then match the sentences to the people.

1 Mo: **A** People _____ the show.

2 Olga: **B** Maybe the other students _____ it.

3 Yero: **C** I hope it _____ tomorrow.

c ✏️ Complete the sentences with *'ll (will)* or *won't*.

1 There'll_____ be lots of food for the buffet, but there _____ be enough cold drinks.

2 It_____ be very hot and sunny tomorrow. I'm sure it _____ rain.

3 People _____ just sit and eat. They _____ dance a lot too.

4 People _____ love the decorations, but they _____ clean up after the party.

2 The *will*-future: questions and short answers

Read the boxes. Then match the questions to the short answers.

Will	I you he/she/it we you they	be there? come? like it?

Yes,	I/you he/she/it we/you/they	will.
No,	I/you he/she/it we/you/they	won't.

1 Will it rain on the day of the school party?
2 Will Mr Chan eat more Jollof rice?
3 Will Jill write the email to the parents?
4 Will the parents bring more food?

A No, he won't.
B Yes, they will.
C No, it won't.
D Yes, she will.

3 The *will*-future: questions with question words

a Read the boxes. Then write the question words in your language.
Check in a dictionary.

Who will come to the party tomorrow?
Where will it be?
What will we do?
When will it be?

English	German	Your language
who?	wer?	_____
what?	was?	_____
where?	wo?	_____
when?	wann?	_____
why?	warum?	_____

b Read the answers. Then complete the questions with the right question words.

What • When • Where • Who

1 _____ will the party start? – I think it'll start at seven o'clock.

2 _____ will we celebrate? – We'll celebrate at the youth club.

3 _____ will you make for the buffet? – I'll make a fruit salad.

4 _____ will be there? – Our friends and classmates will be there.

c Write the questions and complete the answers.

1 When | be home | you | will | ?

   When _____ – I think I'll be home at _____

2 do | What | you | will | ?

   _____ – Maybe I'll _____

4 The *will*-future: making wishes and predictions

a 📖 ✏ Read the blue boxes. Then complete the sentences with phrases
from the green box and *will* or *won't*.

I'm sure the weather will/won't be good.
I hope they'll/won't bring a cake.
Maybe there will/won't be a disco.
I think it will rain.
I don't think it will rain.

With the *will*-future you can say what you
think or know about the future (predictions) or
what you hope for the future (wishes).
You often use phrases like
I think, I hope, Maybe, I'm sure.
⚠ When you make **negative sentences with**
***I think**, you usually say *I don't think … will …*

1 _I'm sure_____ we _____ have school tomorrow.
2 _____ I _____ get a good mark in the English test.
3 _____ it _____ rain today.
4 _____ my cousin _____ visit me at the weekend.

I hope • I'm sure •
Maybe • I think •
I don't think

b 👥 💬 Compare your sentences with a partner.

c 📖 ✏ How will they live in ten years? Read the speech bubbles. Number the pictures (1–3).

1 Maybe I won't be a famous footballer. But I hope I'll be a very good football player.

2 I'm sure I'll be a dancer. Maybe I'll have a dance school.

3 I don't think I'll live in Russia. Maybe I'll live in the US. I hope I'll work at a theatre.

d ✏ What will you do or where will you be in ten years?
Write three sentences or more. Look up more words in a dictionary.

I'm sure	I'll	be	a football player • a teacher • a famous person • …
I hope	I won't	have	a family • children • a shop • a cafe • …
Maybe		live in	England • Germany • Guinea • Syria • …
		…	…
I (don't) think	I'll		

I'm sure I won't be a teacher. But maybe I'll work with children …

e 👥 💬 Compare your sentences with a partner.

5 Conditional sentences (type 1)

a 📖 ✂ ✏ Read the box. Then match the sentence parts.
Mark the simple present and the *will*-future or *can*.

If-clause (condition)	Main clause (result)
If it rains,	we will celebrate inside.
If the weather is good,	we will celebrate outside.
If you like chocolate,	you will like my muffins.
If you don't like meat,	you can have a sandwich.

With conditional 1 sentences you say that something can or will happen in the present or future under a certain condition.
You use the simple present in the *if*-clause and the *will*-future in the main clause. In the main clause, you can also use the modal verb *can*.

1 If it rains at the party,
2 If Mo's group doesn't practise enough,
3 If Jill doesn't write the email now,
4 If the Jollof rice is too spicy for Mr Chan,
5 If you don't like salad,

A he won't like the chilli soup.
B there won't be enough parents to help.
C the dance show won't be good.
D you can bring some snacks or bread.
E the decorations will be ruined.

b 📖 ✏ Read the boxes. Complete the sentences with the right verb forms.
Be careful: The *if*-clause can be at the beginning or the end of the sentence.

1 If you like chocolate, you will like my muffins.

2 You will like my muffins if you like chocolate.

The *if*-clause can go before (1) or after (2) the main clause.
If the *if*-clause goes after the main clause, there is no comma.

1 If Mo's group *practises* (practise) enough, the show _____ (be) great.

2 Many students _____ (dance) if Mo _____ (teach) them the steps.

3 If Mo's group _____ (have) fun, people _____ (have) fun too.

4 People _____ (cheer) a lot if they _____ (like) the show.

5 If people _____ (cheer) a lot, Mo _____ (be) very happy.

If my group practises enough, the show will be great.

c ✏ Write conditional sentences. The *if*-clause can go before or after the main clause.

1 if | you'll be late for school | you don't take the bus

_____

2 if | we can meet at the weekend | I'll help you with maths

_____

3 if | you'll get a better mark in maths | we study together

_____

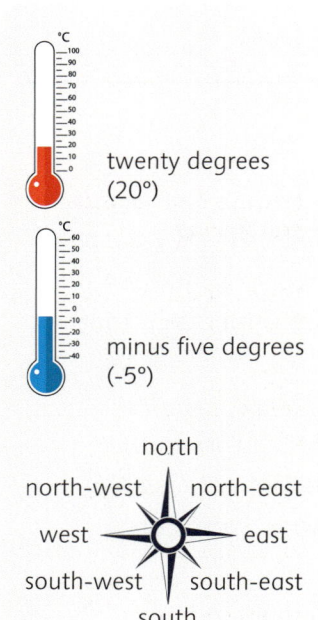

°C
twenty degrees
(20°)

°C
minus five degrees
(-5°)

north
north-west | north-east
west — east
south-west | south-east
south

Talking about the weather:
What will the weather be like tomorrow?

weather forecast
temperature
afternoon temperatures (pl)
degree

English and German

E	G
cold	kalt
sunny	sonnig
windy	windig
warm	warm

rain jacket
jacket
hat
gloves (pl)
umbrella

1 What will the weather be like tomorrow?

a 📖 ✓ Look at the map and read.
Tick the right answer.
The weather forecast is for …

◯ Britain.

◯ Germany.

◯ Europe.

London

b 🔊 85 ✓ Listen to the weather forecast and complete the text.

Tomorrow it will be _____ and _____ in the north of Britain

with afternoon temperatures of about _____ . That's _____

for this time of the year. In the east it _____ cold too, about

_____ . It will be _____ , but it _____ rain.

In London it will be _____ and _____ , about _____ .

2 There's no bad weather, only the wrong clothes!

a 📖 ✂ Look and read. Match the pictures to the weather words.

umbrella   T-shirt   gloves and hat   rain jacket

| rainy and windy | | cold | | rainy and warm | | sunny and hot |

b ✓ Complete the sentences. Use the *will*-future.

a T-shirt | (wear) • my umbrella | (take) • (put) on |
my gloves and hat • (wear) | my rain jacket

1 If it's very sunny and hot, *I'll wear* _____

2 If it's rainy and warm, _____

3 If it's very cold, _____

4 If it's rainy and windy, _____

→ My Words, pp. 106–107

c 🔊 86 📖 Listen and check.

3 Mo's birthday party

spring
summer
autumn
winter

a 🔊 87 Read the questions. Listen and tick.

1 When is Mo's birthday?

◯ in spring   ◯ in summer   ◯ in autumn   ◯ in winter

2 Where will Mo celebrate his birthday?

◯ at the school canteen   ◯ at the youth club   ◯ in the park

3 Will Mo ask all his classmates to come?

◯ Yes, all of them.   ◯ No, no one.   ◯ No, only Olga and Yero.

b What will happen next? Look and read. Write in your exercise book.

1. I think / I'm sure / Maybe there will be ...

Positive and negative statements

⊞
I think the music **will** stop.
I'm sure the music **will** stop.
Maybe the music **will** stop.

⊟
I don't think the music **will** stop.
I'm sure the music **won't** stop.
Maybe the music **won't** stop.

What will happen next?

(to) drop sth.

1

A There will be enough food.
B There won't be enough food.
C … (your idea)

2

A Mo's brother will drop the cake.
B Mo's brother won't drop the cake.
C … (your idea)

3

A Mo will like his aunt's present.
B Mo won't like his aunt's present.
C … (your idea)

4

A The music will stop.
B The music won't stop.
C … (your idea)

c Compare your ideas with a partner.

I think Mo's brother will drop the cake.

I don't agree. I'm sure he won't drop the cake.

→ My Words, pp. 106–107

4 Celebrations in Jill's family

a 🔊 88 ✏️ Listen to three dialogues. Number the pictures (1–3).

New Year's Eve

Diwali

Christmas

b 📑 🔊 88 ✏️ Look and read. Listen again and write the things in the three lists.

presents	fireworks	flowers	candles

traditional costumes	greeting cards	traditional songs	decorations

Diwali: *presents,* _____

_____

Christmas: _____

_____

New Year's Eve: _____

_____

5 Thinking about cultures

a 👥 💬 When does your family celebrate New Year? Talk in a group.

b 👥 ✏️ Collect the dates of your classmates' New Year's celebrations.

c 👥 ✋ Make a festive calendar for your classroom. Add celebrations that are important to you and your classmates.

February
Chinese New Year

May
Sugar Feast

Celebrations and parties:
present
fireworks (pl)
flower
candle
traditional costume
greeting card
song
decoration
New Year

→ My Words, pp. 106–107

6 Your favourite celebration

a ✏ Collect your ideas in the mind map. You can use words from page 102.

TIP: Do some online research if you need more information. You can look up words in an online dictionary.

→ Module 2, p. 26 (Online dictionaries and apps)

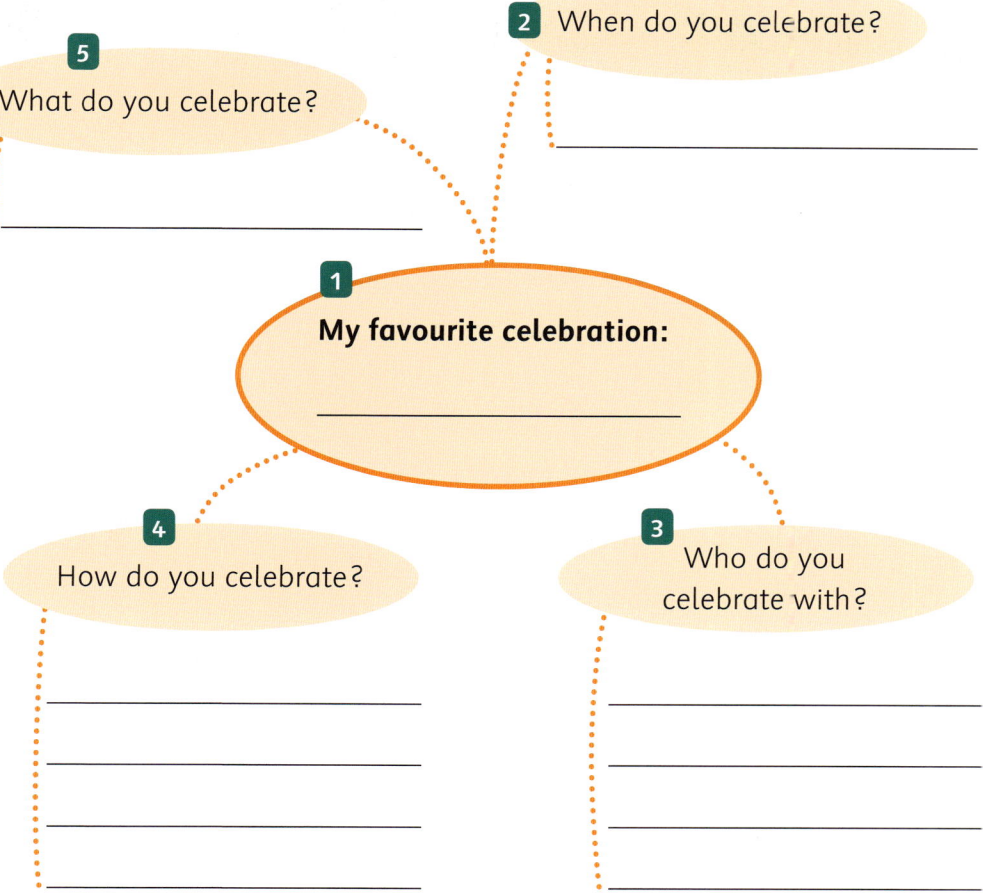

5 What do you celebrate? _____

2 When do you celebrate? _____

1 My favourite celebration: _____

4 How do you celebrate?
_____
_____
_____
_____

3 Who do you celebrate with?
_____
_____
_____
_____

b 👥 💬 Talk to a partner about your ideas.

c ✏ Complete the text with your ideas from 6a. Copy the text in your exercise book. You can add more information.

My favourite celebration

My favourite celebration is _____ (1)

We celebrate it _____ (2)

We celebrate with _____ (3)

We _____ (4)

_____

_____ celebrates _____ (5)

_____

d 💬 Present your text in class.

→ My Words, pp. 106–107

1 How to make a mind map

a 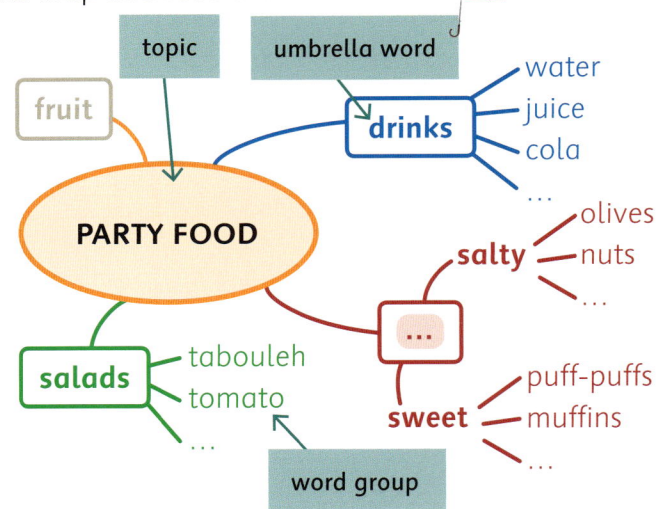 ✏️ Look at the mind map and read the boxes.
Tick the right answers.

A **mind map** can help you to structure your ideas. Think of a **topic**: *my favourite food, school subjects,* … Collect your ideas and write them on a piece of paper. Make **word groups** and find **umbrella words** for your word groups. Draw your mind map.

1 What's the topic of this mind map?

◯ My favourite food   ◯ Party food   ◯ Drinks

2 What's the missing umbrella word (…)?

◯ hot drinks   ◯ sweets   ◯ snacks

3 Which two words can you add to the umbrella word *salads*?

◯ fruit   ◯ cake   ◯ soup   ◯ potato   ◯ tea

b ✏️ Make a mind map about your dream party. Read and write.

1. Collect ideas for the topic *My dream party*.

| celebrate with all friends • listen to cool music • dance • … |

2. Make word groups and write down umbrella words for your word groups. You can choose umbrella words from the box.

| decorations • drinks • food • games and activities • music • place • … |

3. Write the topic in the middle of the page. Write down the umbrella words and connect them to the topic.

4. Write down the word groups and connect them to the umbrella words.

c ✏️ 💬 With the help of your mind map, write a short text or give a short talk about your dream party.
My dream party takes place on the beach. All my friends are there. We're listening to cool music …

Checkpoint

1 ✏ Write down the right umbrella word for each word group.

clothes • weather • vegetables

_____
bell pepper, carrot, cucumber, tomato

_____
T-shirt, trousers, skirt, pullover

_____
sunny, cloudy, windy, rainy, hot, cold

😊 ⬜ 😐 ⬜ ☹ ⬜

2 🔊 89 ✏ Look and listen. Complete the text.

Tomorrow it _____ rainy and _____ in the _____ of Britain. The afternoon _____ will only be _____ . In the _____ it will be warmer, about _____ . It will be _____ in the morning, but _____ in the afternoon. In the _____ and south-west it _____ at about _____ .

London

😊 ⬜ 😐 ⬜ ☹ ⬜

3 ✏ Complete the questions with question words.

1 _____ will our class party start? – It'll start at three o'clock.

2 _____ will we celebrate? – I think we'll celebrate in the park.

3 _____ will be there? – All our classmates will be there, I hope.

4 _____ will we do there? – I think we'll play volleyball and have a picnic.

5 _____ will we eat? – We'll have cold snacks and salads for the picnic.

😊 ⬜ 😐 ⬜ ☹ ⬜

4 ✏ Complete the sentences with the right verb forms.

1 If it _____ (be) sunny on Saturday, we _____ (go) to the park.

2 If we _____ (be) enough people, we _____ (play) football.

3 We _____ (have) a picnic if people _____ (bring) some food.

4 If we _____ (not have) enough food, we _____ (buy) a pizza.

😊 ⬜ 😐 ⬜ ☹ ⬜

English	German	My notes
I hope the weather will be good.	Ich hoffe, dass das Wetter gut wird.	
Maybe the other students won't like the dance show.	Vielleicht werden die anderen Schüler die Tanzshow nicht mögen.	
Will there be enough parents to help?	Werden genug Eltern da sein, um zu helfen?	
I'll send the email right now.	Ich schicke die Email jetzt gleich.	
How will Mr Chan like my Jollof rice?	Wie wird Herrn Chan mein Jollof-Reis schmecken?	
If it **rains**, the decorations **will be** ruined.	Wenn es regnet, wird die Dekoration kaputtgehen.	
If your Jollof rice **is** too spicy for Mr Chan, he **can** eat your puff-puffs.	Wenn dein Jollof-Reis für Herrn Chan zu scharf ist, kann er deine Puff-Puffs essen.	
Let's celebrate.	Lass(t) uns feiern.	

Celebrations and parties:	**Feiern und Partys:**	
decoration	die Dekoration	
food	das Essen	
buffet	das Büfett	
show	die Show	
party, *pl* parties	die Party, *(Pl.)* die Partys	
present	das Geschenk	
fireworks *(pl)*	das Feuerwerk; die Feuerwerkskörper *(Pl.)*	
flower	die Blume	
candle	die Kerze	
traditional costume	das traditionelle Kostüm	
greeting card	die Grußkarte	
song	das Lied	
New Year	(das) Neujahr	
(to) celebrate outside/inside	draußen/drinnen feiern	

My Words

English	German	My notes
Wishes and predictions (Wünsche und Vorhersagen)		
I think it will rain.	Ich glaube, dass es regnen wird.	
I don't think it will rain.	Ich glaube nicht, dass es regnen wird.	
I'm sure it will (won't) …	Ich bin sicher, dass es (nicht) …	
I hope it will (won't) …	Ich hoffe, dass es (nicht) …	
Maybe it will (won't) …	Ich hoffe, dass es (nicht) …	
(to) forget (about) sth.	etwas vergessen	
(to) drop sth.	etwas fallen lassen	
I'm worried about …	Ich mache mir Sorgen über …	
Don't worry.	Mach dir keine Sorgen. / Macht euch keine Sorgen.	
What will happen next?	Was wird als nächstes passieren?	
It's perfect/OK/bad for a party when it's sunny.	Es ist perfekt/OK/schlecht für eine Party, wenn es sonnig ist.	
What will the weather be like tomorrow?	Wie wird das Wetter morgen sein?	
It'll be sunny and warm.	Es wird sonnig und warm sein.	
Talking about the weather (Über das Wetter sprechen) **cloudy** bewölkt • **cold** kalt • **cool** kühl • **hot** heiß • **rainy** regnerisch • **sunny** sonnig • **warm** warm • **windy** windig • **temperature** die Temperatur • **afternoon temperatures** die Temperaturen am Nachmittag • **degree** der Grad • **twenty degrees (20°)** zwanzig Grad • **minus five degrees (-5°)** minus fünf Grad • **(to) rain** regnen • **weather forecast** die Wetter-vorhersage **east** der Osten; östlich • **north** der Norden; nördlich • **south** der Süden; südlich • **west** der Westen; westlich		
spring	der Frühling	
summer	der Sommer	
autumn	der Herbst	
winter	der Winter	
Clothes (Kleidung) **gloves** (pl) die Handschuhe (Pl.) • **hat** die Mütze; der Hut • **jacket** die Jacke • **rain jacket** die Regenjacke • **umbrella** der Regenschirm; der Sonnenschirm		

infinitive	simple past	past participle	German
be [biː]	was [wɒz]	been [biːn]	sein; war; (ist) gewesen
buy [baɪ]	bought [bɔːt]	bought [bɔːt]	kaufen; kaufte; (hat) gekauft
come [kʌm]	came [keɪm]	come [kʌm]	kommen; kam; (ist) gekommen
cut [kʌt]	cut [kʌt]	cut [kʌt]	schneiden; schnitt; (hat) geschnitten
do [duː]	did [dɪd]	done [dʌn]	tun; tat; (hat) getan
drink [drɪŋk]	drank [dræŋk]	drunk [drʌŋk]	trinken; trank; (hat) getrunken
eat [iːt]	ate [et, eɪt]	eaten ['iːtn]	essen; aß; (hat) gegessen
forget [fə'get]	forgot [fə'gɒt]	forgotten [fə'gɒtn]	vergessen; vergaß; (hat) vergessen
get [get]	got [gɒt]	got [gɒt]	bekommen; bekam; (hat) bekommen
go [gəʊ]	went [went]	gone [gɒn]	gehen; ging; (ist) gegangen
have [hæv]	had [hæd]	had [hæd]	haben; hatte; (hat) gehabt
lie [laɪ]	lay [leɪ]	lain [leɪn]	liegen; lag; (hat) gelegen
make [meɪk]	made [meɪd]	made [meɪd]	machen; machte; (hat) gemacht
meet [miːt]	met [met]	met [met]	treffen; traf; (hat) getroffen

infinitive	simple past	past participle	German
put [pʊt]	put [pʊt]	put [pʊt]	legen, stellen; legte, stellte; (hat) gelegt, (hat) gestellt
read [riːd]	read [red]	read [red]	lesen; las; (hat) gelesen
see [siː]	saw [sɔː]	seen [siːn]	sehen; sah; (hat) gesehen
sew [səʊ]	sewed [səʊd]	sewn [səʊn]	nähen; nähte; (hat) genäht
sit [sɪt]	sat [sæt]	sat [sæt]	sitzen; saß; (hat) gesessen
speak [spiːk]	spoke [spəʊk]	spoken ['spəʊkən]	sprechen; sprach; (hat) gesprochen
stand [stænd]	stood [stʊd]	stood [stʊd]	stehen; stand; (hat) gestanden
take [teɪk]	took [tʊk]	taken ['teɪkən]	nehmen; nahm; (hat) genommen
teach [tiːtʃ]	taught [tɔːt]	taught [tɔːt]	unterrichten; unterrichtete; (hat) unterrichtet
tell [tel]	told [təʊld]	told [təʊld]	erzählen, berichten; erzählte, berichtete; (hat) erzählt, (hat) berichtet
think [θɪŋk]	thought [θɔːt]	thought [θɔːt]	denken; dachte; (hat) gedacht
wear [weə]	wore [wɔː]	worn [wɔːn]	tragen; trug; (hat) getragen
win [wɪn]	won [wɒn]	won [wɒn]	gewinnen; gewann; (hat) gewonnen

English sounds

[iː]	green, he, sea		[b]	bike, table, verb
[ɑː]	ask, class, car, park		[p]	pen, paper, shop
[ɔː]	or, ball, door, four, morning		[d]	day, window, good
[uː]	ruler, blue, too, two, you		[t]	ten, letter, at
[ɜː]	early, her, girl, work, T-shirt		[g]	go, again, bag
[ɪ]	in, big, expensive		[k]	kitchen, car, back
[e]	yes, bed, again, breakfast		[m]	man, remember, mum
[æ]	animal, apple, black, cat		[n]	no, one, ten
[ʌ]	mum, bus, colour		[ŋ]	wrong, young, uncle, thanks
[ɒ]	song, on, dog, what		[l]	like, old, small
[ʊ]	book, good, pullover		[r]	ruler, friend, sorry
[ə]	again, today, a sister		[w]	we, where, one
[i]	happy, monkey		[j]	yes, you, uniform
			[f]	family, after, laugh
[eɪ]	name, eight, play, great		[v]	very, seven, have
[aɪ]	I, time, right, my		[s]	six, poster, yes
[ɔɪ]	boy, toilet, noise		[z]	zoo, quiz, his, music, please
[əʊ]	old, no, road, yellow		[ʃ]	she, station, English
[aʊ]	now, house		[ʒ]	usually, revision, garage
[eə]	where, pair, share, their		[tʃ]	child, teacher, watch
[ʊə]	tour		[dʒ]	job, German, project, orange
			[θ]	thing, three, bathroom, both
			[ð]	the, father, with
			[h]	house, who, behind

The English alphabet

A, a	[eɪ]	H, h	[eɪtʃ]	O, o	[əʊ]	V, v	[viː]
B, b	[biː]	I, i	[aɪ]	P, p	[piː]	W, w	['dʌbljuː]
C, c	[siː]	J, j	[dʒeɪ]	Q, q	[kjuː]	X, x	[eks]
D, d	[diː]	K, k	[keɪ]	R, r	[ɑː]	Y, y	[waɪ]
E, e	[iː]	L, l	[el]	S, s	[es]	Z, z	[zed]
F, f	[ef]	M, m	[em]	T, t	[tiː]		
G, g	[dʒiː]	N, n	[en]	U, u	[juː]		

Numbers

English numbers

0	oh, zero [əʊ, ˈzɪərəʊ]			
1	one [wʌn]	1st	first [fɜːst]	
2	two [tuː]	2nd	second [ˈsekənd]	
3	three [θriː]	3rd	third [θɜːd]	
4	four [fɔː]	4th	fourth [fɔːθ]	
5	five [faɪv]	5th	fifth [fɪfθ]	
6	six [sɪks]	6th	sixth [sɪksθ]	
7	seven [ˈsevn]	7th	seventh [ˈsevnθ]	
8	eight [eɪt]	8th	eighth [eɪtθ]	
9	nine [naɪn]	9th	ninth [naɪnθ]	
10	ten [ten]	10th	tenth [tenθ]	
11	eleven [ɪˈlevn]	11th	eleventh [ɪˈlevnθ]	
12	twelve [twelv]	12th	twelfth [twelfθ]	
13	thirteen [θɜːˈtiːn]	13th	thirteenth [θɜːˈtiːnθ]	
14	fourteen [fɔːˈtiːn]	14th	fourteenth [fɔːˈtiːnθ]	
15	fifteen [fɪfˈtiːn]	15th	fifteenth [fɪfˈtiːnθ]	
16	sixteen [sɪksˈtiːn]	16th	sixteenth [sɪksˈtiːnθ]	
17	seventeen [sevnˈtiːn]	17th	seventeenth [sevnˈtiːnθ]	
18	eighteen [eɪˈtiːn]	18th	eighteenth [eɪˈtiːnθ]	
19	nineteen [naɪnˈtiːn]	19th	nineteenth [naɪnˈtiːnθ]	
20	twenty [ˈtwenti]	20th	twentieth [ˈtwentiəθ]	
21	twenty-one [twentiˈwʌn]	21st	twenty-first [twentiˈfɜːst]	
22	twenty-two [twentiˈtuː]	22nd	twenty-second [twentiˈsekənd]	
23	twenty-three [twentiˈθriː]	23rd	twenty-third [twentiˈθɜːd]	
…		…		
30	thirty [ˈθɜːti]	30th	thirtieth [ˈθɜːtiəθ]	
40	forty [ˈfɔːti]	40th	fortieth [ˈfɔːtiəθ]	
50	fifty [ˈfɪfti]	50th	fiftieth [ˈfɪftiəθ]	
60	sixty [ˈsɪksti]	60th	sixtieth [ˈsɪkstiəθ]	
70	seventy [ˈsevnti]	70th	seventieth [ˈsevntiəθ]	
80	eighty [ˈeɪti]	80th	eightieth [ˈeɪtiəθ]	
90	ninety [ˈnaɪnti]	90th	ninetieth [ˈnaɪntiəθ]	
100	a/one hundred [ə/wʌn ˈhʌndrəd]	100th	hundredth [ˈhʌndrədθ]	
101	one hundred and one	101st	hundred and first	
102	one hundred and two	102nd	hundred and second	
…		…		

Classroom English

You and your teacher

Good morning, Mr/Mrs …

Good afternoon, Mr/Mrs …

Can I open/close the window, please?

Can I go to the toilet, please?

Goodbye. See you tomorrow.

Du und dein Lehrer/deine Lehrerin

Guten Morgen, Herr/Frau …

Guten Tag, Herr/Frau …

Kann ich bitte das Fenster öffnen/zumachen?

Kann ich bitte zur Toilette gehen?

Auf Wiedersehen. Bis morgen.

Homework and exercises

I don't understand this exercise.

Sorry, I don't know.

What's for homework?

Can I work with Nour?

Hausaufgaben und Übungen

Ich verstehe die Übung nicht.

Es tut mir leid, das weiß ich nicht.

Was haben wir als Hausaufgabe auf?

Kann ich mit Nour arbeiten?

You need help

Can you help me, please?

What's … in English/German?

Can I say it in German?

Can you say/play that again, please?

Du brauchst Hilfe

Können Sie mir bitte helfen?

Was heißt … auf Englisch/Deutsch?

Kann ich das auf Deutsch sagen?

Können Sie das bitte noch einmal sagen/abspielen?

What your teacher says

Listen, please.

Quiet, please.

Open your books at page 24, please.

Look at picture A.

Do exercise 5 for homework, please.

Where's your book/exercise book?

That's very good.

Correct the mistakes.

Make a poster about …

That's all for today. You can go.

Was dein Lehrer/deine Lehrerin sagt

Hört bitte zu.

Ruhe bitte.

Schlagt bitte Seite 24 auf.

Seht euch Bild A an.

Macht bitte Übung 5 als Hausaufgabe.

Wo ist dein Buch/Übungsheft?

Das ist sehr gut.

Korrigiert die Fehler.

Macht ein Poster zum Thema …

Das ist alles für heute. Ihr könnt gehen.